PRAISE FOR
Beauty of Aging

Karen O'Connor's recipe for aging is keep going and keep growing, both humanly and spiritually. As an oldster myself, I would say she's got it right.

J. I. PACKER
PROFESSOR OF THEOLOGY
REGENT COLLEGE
VANCOUVER, B.C., CANADA

I was very impressed with the down-to-earth writing and suggestions of Karen O'Connor in her book *The Beauty of Aging.* I was both confronted with improvements I needed to make in my own maturing process and encouraged by other aspects of her writing. Thank you, Karen, for writing a book that is dedicated to us older women who want to age with grace, gratitude and grit.

ANNA HAYFORD
WIFE OF PASTOR JACK W. HAYFORD

Oh, how I wish I were not at the place in life where I am invited to offer comments on a book about aging. But alas, I am. Why are we so afraid of aging and so bent on clinging to our youth? For me, I think it is because we have not had good role models for aging gracefully. I always feared turning into my grandmother, with her rolled down hose and her "sausage roll" hair—secured with a hairnet. For today's baby boomers who have passed the 50-mark, Karen O'Connor provides an excellent role model of what it looks like to age beautifully. Her wisdom could make even the young look forward to being senior citizens! She shows how to do it right—and I should know! After all, there's more to aging than AARP discounts!

FLORENCE LITTAUER
FOUNDER OF THE CLASSeminar
AT 78, STILL A SPEAKER AND AUTHOR, *PERSONALITY PLUS* AND *SILVER BOXES*

The Beauty *of* Aging

Karen O'Connor

Regal

From Gospel Light
Ventura, California, U.S.A.

Regal

PUBLISHED BY REGAL BOOKS
FROM GOSPEL LIGHT
VENTURA, CALIFORNIA, U.S.A.
PRINTED IN THE U.S.A.

Regal Books is a ministry of Gospel Light, a Christian publisher dedicated to serving the local church. We believe God's vision for Gospel Light is to provide church leaders with biblical, user-friendly materials that will help them evangelize, disciple and minister to children, youth and families.

It is our prayer that this Regal book will help you discover biblical truth for your own life and help you meet the needs of others. May God richly bless you.

Library of Congress Cataloging-in-Publication Data
O'Connor, Karen, 1938-
  The beauty of aging / Karen O'Connor.
    p. cm.
  ISBN 0-8307-4277-8 (trade paper)
  1. Older Christians—Prayer-books and devotions—English. 2. Older women—Prayer-books and devotions—English. I. Title.
  BV4580.O353 2006
  242'.65—dc22   2006011063

1   2   3   4   5   6   7   8   9   10   /   10   09   08   07   06

Rights for publishing this book in other languages are contracted by Gospel Light Worldwide, the international nonprofit ministry of Gospel Light. Gospel Light Worldwide also provides publishing and technical assistance to international publishers dedicated to producing Sunday School and Vacation Bible School curricula and books in the languages of the world.

FOR JUNE

Contents

A Word from the Author

I believe God is managing affairs and that He doesn't need any advice from me," Henry Ford once said. "With God in charge, I believe everything will work out for the best in the end. So what is there to worry about?"

As we age, there are increasing responsibilities, opportunities and challenges. If we didn't know that God is at the helm, we'd be overwhelmed at every turn. But He is, and so we can truly be still and know that He is God (see Ps. 46:10).

With this truth to anchor us, growing older is a lot easier and more satisfying. Take a deep breath and let it happen. I hope this book will help you do just that, and perhaps bring to you a smile, a tear, a sigh, an "aha!" We're all in this together.

The book is divided into seven sections: Faith, Family, Friends, Food, Fitness, Finances and Fun. I invite you to look at each one, how it relates to you as you grow older and how to make this season in your life a beautiful and satisfying one because you accept the blessings and the burdens with grace, greet all of life with gratitude and stand up with grit when stuff happens. Knowing that God is in charge and that He will guide, guard and govern you right through your last breath—and beyond—makes all the difference. We needn't fear the future—for God is already there!

Karen O'Connor
San Diego, California

Section 1

FAITH

WE LIVE BY FAITH, NOT BY SIGHT.
2 CORINTHIANS 5:7

As I look back on my life, I did just the opposite of what the apostle Paul taught. I lived by sight, not by faith. All my choices and decisions were based on what I felt, on what I noticed and on what I heard and saw in the world. And I held my own point of view in high regard—until the crisis of an unwanted divorce knocked me down.

I lay there as still as a stone. I had no resources, no help, no answers—until a counselor friend asked me a disturbing question: "How are you and God getting along?"

What kind of a question is that? I couldn't respond. I hadn't even thought about God except when I said a mere "thank you" before a meal. But that question would not let go of me. It started a journey that led me to Jesus Christ—His teachings, His promises, His friendship—and to the knowledge that to walk with Christ *is* to live by faith, not by sight—in marriage, in parenting, in friendship, in work—and to ask for His grace when I fail.

Author Peter De Vries says it well: "It takes a lot more faith to live this life without faith than with it." The writings in this section reflect how living by faith is even more important as we grow older.

Row, Row, Row Your *Own* Boat!

As a kid, one of my favorite summertime activities was sitting on the back of Uncle Bud's "woody" station wagon. Legs dangling and arms around each other's shoulders, my cousins and I sat in the woody as it bumped and skidded over the dirt and gravel roads to Lake Wauconda—just down the road from the family's summer cottage. Those were the days before seat belts and air bags. Less safe then, but lots more fun!

Then came the best time of all—going for a ride in Uncle Bud's freshly painted row boat. The shiny oars sparkled in the sun as we lowered them into the water and then took turns rowing our way across the lake.

Uncle Bud sat in back, barking orders when we got distracted watching other boaters or became too giddy. "Pay attention to what you're doing," he shouted. "Row your own boat. That way, no one gets hurt."

I remember giggling when I first heard him say that. How could we possibly row someone else's boat? He explained what he meant. "Keep your mind and your eyes on what you're doing. Be responsible for your actions, and you'll be fun and have fun."

I hadn't thought about that sage advice for 50 years or more—until last month when my husband, Charles, and I took a cruise to Alaska. The first evening, we were seated in the dining room at a table with another married couple, Edie and John. We enjoyed getting to know them as they shared details about their family, their marriage of seven years—the second for each of them—and their life in a new home on a lake in Indiana, where they had recently moved. As they talked about the pleasure of lakeside living, I was suddenly reminded of those carefree summers of long ago at Lake Wauconda.

Then the most amazing thing occurred. Edie talked about a situation in their family that was painful and disappointing. I leaned forward, finding it easy to empathize with her, as some of the things she shared were similar to events in my life.

When Edie finished, she took a sip of water and sat back in silence. I was about to comment, to ask how she managed such a challenge, when she piped up again. "It's not in our boat," she said, smiling.

John looked on, patted her shoulder tenderly and agreed. "That's right. It's not in our boat. We're learning to take care of what's in our own boat and leaving other people—even if they are related to us—to take care of what's in theirs."

I felt as though I were listening to Uncle Bud all over again. "Row your own boat." Hands off other boats. So be it. Amen!

Oh, but it's much easier and more fun to row someone else's boat! I find that this is especially true as I grow older. I have so much wisdom to offer my friends and family (why, I'm a legend in my own mind!), and I love to look through their belongings, to pick and choose what I think they should keep and what to toss overboard, and to take some of their stuff into my boat so that they won't have to row so hard. I can come up with a list of suggestions a mile long for how to row smoothly, if only they'd ask me.

They don't usually, but that doesn't stop me from offering my advice anyway—or being tempted to—and then wondering why they turn away or cut back on our time together. Alas! I am my own worst enemy—the pirate at the helm, ready to take over someone else's ship, while my own is sinking.

And what does all this have to do with faith? Everything! When I row for others or take their burdens and put them in my boat (children who have left the church, a relative living a lesbian lifestyle, a couple living together outside of marriage), I am doing for them what only they (and God) can do. I am assuming that I know more about how to resolve their problems than God does.

But most important, I am taking my eyes off rowing my own boat and maintaining the things that I am called to carry. A collision, a man overboard, a sinking is surely inevitable if I keep this up. So today, with the eyes of faith, I will row my own boat and support others with prayer and love in rowing theirs—regardless of what I see with my human eyes.

GRACE
Surely you desire truth in the inner parts; you teach me wisdom in the inmost place.
(Psalm 51:6)

GRATITUDE
Lord, I thank You with a full heart for the gift of faith.

GRIT
Today, I will toss overboard what belongs to others, take stock of what to keep in my own boat and then row as God leads.

Easy Rhythms

I read some time ago that Billy Graham reads five psalms a day. By doing so, he can move through all 150 in one month. I was so inspired by this practice that I adopted it myself, although I've not been consistent, I'm sorry to admit. Some days I put it off until later and then get distracted or forget. I don't want to lean on these excuses any longer. I want to be as faithful at reading a psalm each day as I am at taking my daily vitamins.

Today is the perfect day to start fresh. It's the last day of December. Tomorrow will be the first day of a new year. Instead of setting goals such as sticking to the perfect diet, getting the latest speaking engagement or book contract, or having the ideal income, what if I began by setting a goal of reading at least one psalm each day? And not necessarily in the order it appears in the Bible. What if I made it a joyful excursion into God's Word, instead of a chore that had to be completed before I could read the daily newspaper without feeling guilty?

What if I consider it an opportunity rather than a rule? What if I live the coming year in an easy rhythm of conversation with God, inspired by the psalms? Maybe I'd realize, as David did, that all the wisdom I need is in the high tower of the Almighty. There I'll find faith and forgiveness, mercy and love, strength and grace.

I'm getting excited just thinking about it. I'm going to do it. And if I slip, it will be all right. I can start again. It's not about perfection. It's about being willing. I'm willing.

I'm going to get a jump on it right now. Why wait another day? Today can be the first day of *my* new year of faith. I'm going to begin with one of my favorite psalms. I'll read it and add a few notes.

Psalm 121

I lift up my eyes to the hills—

where does my help come from?

Every day, I look at the hills to the east of where I live. Over the years, I've hiked the trails, rested on the grassy slopes and waded in the streams of those hills. Those gold and green hills always turn my heart to our creator.

My help comes from the LORD,
the Maker of heaven and earth.

And the maker of my soul. *He* is my only hope and salvation. I trust in Him alone.

He will not let your foot slip—
he who watches over you will not slumber;

He protects me whether I am awake or asleep. His eye is always on me, day and night. He is not distracted or forgetful or negligent. He never loses interest in me. He never ever grows weary. I put my faith in Him.

Indeed, he who watches over Israel
will neither slumber nor sleep.

Window Washer

"**M**om," our daughter Erin sobbed into the phone. "Why are we so far away from each other? We're all getting older, and we should be together. We love you and Charles so much. Would you consider moving closer?"

"Honey," I stammered, as my stomach clutched, "the . . . just the . . . the very thought is overwhelming. We planned to be in San Diego for the rest of our days and . . ." I listed all the reasons why it didn't make sense to relocate at our age.

"I'm not sure why I feel nudged to ask you at this time, but I do. Please, Mom, would you pray about it?" She paused, then added the kicker: "A brand-new community of homes for people over 55 is going up right near us. It's going to be beautiful. The builder has a great reputation in this area, and the homes will be environmentally friendly and . . ."

She had touched my soft spot. My head reeled.

"Of course, we'll pray. I don't want to miss a leading from God. But it doesn't sound feasible . . ." I heard myself rattling on, trying to bury the discomfort with words. We said good-bye with the promise to pray, and then I burst into tears. "God, are You in cahoots with Erin behind my back?"

I looked at my plan for the new year. I had a book due in March (this one). We were planning to take a trip to Denver in July and go camping in Mammoth in August. We had signed up for a cruise in September, and we wanted to fit in a trip to Ohio and Kentucky to see other family members.

Christmas this year was right around the corner, and relatives were on their way. I was getting over the flu and had a stack of work on my desk to complete before New Year's Day. "Surely, God," I prayed, "You're not asking me to squeeze in a major move next year when my calendar is already packed?"

But I had promised that I'd pray and so I did—sort of. God might call it something else—like interrogation. My husband prayed, too. We talked to God privately and together and finally sought His will through listening prayer—whereby we spoke aloud what was on our hearts and then listened for a response.

As I waited, two words rose up in my mind in large uppercase letters: "REST" and "TRUST." That was it—no conversation, no direction, no assurance one way or the other. So I rested and tried to trust. But then I jumped up, paced around the house, talked too much, cried and murmured to Charles all my fears and worries. Then I rested again and took another stab at trusting. I noticed how controlling I am! And how set in my ways I can be. The older I get, the more set I am. I've also noticed this in other people as they age. They don't like disruption, change or inconvenience.

And so it went for days. Finally, I let it all go. The stress was killing me. If we were to move, we'd hear about it; if we were to stay, we'd hear that, too. I began to sleep again and eat without upsetting my stomach.

A few days later my husband spoke up. "It looks like we're moving to Watsonville."

"We are? How can you be sure?" I looked him in the eye. It wasn't like Charles to be definite so soon about such a big decision. He had been adamant against moving when we first talked about it.

We prayed again and continued to pray every morning thereafter, focusing on this one issue. Within a few days, we felt led to look into the new community. We visited the builder's website, spoke with the sales agent and asked for a packet of materials to study. A day later, we put down a deposit on one of the lots. Out of 74 homes still in the framing stage, only 14 were left. We got the one we wanted! We were ecstatic. It seemed the Lord had spoken to both of us.

But then the regret, worry, fear and anxiety moved in, big time. I couldn't sleep. I started crying again. I was overcome by the love and tears my close friends expressed when I told them our news. And on it went, one day up, the next one down. I could barely eat again, and I woke up in the night terrified that we hadn't heard the Lord correctly and that we were in the midst of making a huge mistake.

We continued to pray and to take the next indicated step and the next and the next. The more we rested and trusted and then stepped forward, the more strength and grace and faith we received. We were finally able to be sad and happy, eager and nostalgic at the same time. We learned to *be* with our feelings instead of running from them. God was there with us. I knew it.

It was as though He had washed my window on life and then thrown it open and sent forth a gust of cleansing wind. He was shifting my point of view. I would no longer look at life in the same way or from the same perspective.

"It can be easy to have tunnel vision if we are never exposed to other perspectives, if we never even take time to look," writes Nancy Carmichael in her article "Windows in

My House."[1] It was as though she were speaking directly to me over a cup of tea in my kitchen. Did I have tunnel vision? Maybe so. I enjoyed my current home. I didn't want to move. I didn't like the idea of anyone—including my daughter, whom I love—messing things up. I had carved out a lifestyle that suited me just fine, and I was committed to it—until that day when the phone rang and the sob of love and petition seared my soul.

I haven't been the same since. I can't go back to my old way of seeing or thinking. I can't hide behind my age. The great Window Washer has cleansed my point of view and changed the view itself. I'll be looking at the beautiful Santa Cruz Mountains from my new windows and only remembering what it was like to view Mission Bay from my former ones.

And so, we are moving north to a new house with new windows in every room. Everything outside them will be new—new friends, new church, new gym, new malls, new highways, new neighbors, a new way of being with my family—and with my God.

> Stand at the crossroads and look; ask for the ancient paths, ask where the good way is, and walk in it, and you will find rest for your souls (Jer. 6:16).

REST and TRUST! And so I am resting and trusting— at last—by faith *and* by sight. For the view is much clearer now that God has washed my window on the world.

GRACE

Each of you should look not only to your own
interests, but also to the interests of others.
(Philippians 2:4)

GRATITUDE

Lord, thank You for washing the window of my soul.

GRIT

Today, I will choose to look through the window
of *Your* will, regardless of the circumstances.

Note

1. Nancy Carmichael, "Windows in My House," *Woman's Touch* (May/June
   2001), p. 25.

Straw Prayers

As I grow older, things of the world are losing their appeal. I don't care as much as I used to about shopping or eating out or going to a movie. But I love to walk hand in hand with my husband or a grandchild and watch the sun set. I enjoy tossing up bits of bread at the park and watching the gulls swoop and caw and then snatch them out of the air. I like to relax on the deck with a glass of lemonade and my journal.

I'm drawn to different kinds of books than I used to be. I'm reading works by some of the classic Christian writers, such as Hannah Whitall Smith, A. W. Tozer and Andrew Murray.

While browsing through a bookstore some time ago, I picked up a copy of *The Practice of the Presence of God*. I'd heard of it, but I'd never read it. And I didn't know anything about the author, Brother Lawrence, born Nicolas Herman in 1605. I leafed through the book on the spot and knew that I had to buy it. I've read it several times now and have colored the pages with highlights and asterisks and notations.

How curious that a man who lived four centuries before I was born would have so much to say that I needed to hear. Nicolas was raised a Catholic and, as a teenager, joined the French army when the French crown joined with the German Protestants to attack the Catholic government of the Holy Roman Empire. He was severely wounded in battle and held as a prisoner of war. Nicolas partially recovered and then went to work for a local treasury official, Mr. Fieubert.

During the winter of his eighteenth year, Nicolas stopped one day to look at a bare tree. He began thinking about how in a short time leaves would appear again on the tree, followed by flowers and fruit. He was suddenly aware of the presence and power of God who created this amazing process!

Nicolas decided to dedicate himself to God as he continued his life and work. Over time, however, he became dissatisfied with the world. Finally, at age 50, he joined a Carmelite monastery in Paris to find refuge and peace. He took the name Brother Lawrence and kept it until his death.

Brother Lawrence looked forward to serving God in some great way. Much to his disappointment, however, he was put in charge of the kitchen—the last place he wanted to be! The monotony of preparing meals and washing dishes was not the high call he had hoped for. But he accepted it, assuming that God assigned this duty to chasten him. To Brother Lawrence's surprise, however, just the opposite occurred. He was later quoted as saying that God "disappointed" him by giving him a life filled with joy!

So kitchen duty it was. Brother Lawrence decided to make his work count for something in Christ's kingdom. He would do every task, regardless of how menial—even picking up a straw from the floor—as an act of faith and love for God, as a prayer of praise and thanksgiving. It took time to develop this attitude of heart, but Brother Lawrence was committed to doing so.

Soon, others noticed the change in this unseemly man of God, and they started asking for his secret. Surely, they thought, he must have a certain method or routine or a list of prayers that resulted in his humble attitude and peaceful countenance. Brother Lawrence's reputation spread to religious leaders from all walks of life—though he rarely set foot beyond the borders of the monastery.

In a time when there were no DVD players, no radios, no televisions, no Internet, and no telephones or fax machines, Brother Lawrence became a kind of celebrity—without any self-promotion or publicity. He simply practiced the presence of God in all his affairs. Clearly, he had something that others wanted.

Even the Abbot of Beaufort, a monk of prestige at the time, wrote endless letters asking Brother Lawrence for spiritual counsel and direction for his own life! The two men exchanged 15 letters and met 4 times to discuss what Brother Lawrence had learned by focusing his mind on the constant presence of God in everyday life.

The abbot, eager for the secret to Brother Lawrence's spiritual success, recorded their conversations and later edited them, along with the letters, to create the book known today as *The Practice of the Presence of God*. The abbot published the book in the mid-1690s, just after Brother Lawrence died at age 84, following only two weeks of illness—this during a time in history when the average life span was about 40 years!

The book sold well after publication, and sales have remained constant for the past 400 years. All this without a media tour, a website, TV appearances, radio interviews and bookstore autograph parties. And Brother Lawrence certainly did not have a speaking platform—something that is required today by most publishers.

His experience was not a one-time feeling or a method of prayer or meditation but simply a way of life, a practice. In fact, Brother Lawrence claimed that when he accepted advice from others or tried to live with a plan for spiritual growth, he only became frustrated and confused. So he went back to practicing the presence, and then everything fell into place.

He concentrated on God each moment, regardless of the circumstances. Everything in his life was secondary to his relationship with the Almighty. To Brother Lawrence, living in the presence of God was not a matter of going to church, saying a certain prayer or being faithful to some method. In fact, he shunned all forms of human piety—except those actions required of him as a monk.

He did not abuse his body, as many saints of his day were known to do. He did not deprive himself of sleep or food. He simply delighted himself in the Lord, and when he found his mind wandering, he stopped, repented and started again. He did not want to waste a moment focused on himself and his sin when he could be in the presence of God.

Brother Lawrence was governed by love. Even washing a dish for the love of God excited him. He was guided by the truth. He knew that he was saved by grace alone, so he didn't fret about sin. He confessed and moved on. He saw too many people wasting time with self-induced piety or complaints or self-judgment. He avoided all of that. His focus was God and God alone.

He was quick to admit that he was a sinner like everyone else. But he knew that God forgives. He acknowledged over and over that he could not go it alone, so he didn't even try. The moment he sinned, he stopped, confessed, received forgiveness and took up his life again, loving God.

Brother Lawrence behaved toward the Lord with the greatest simplicity, speaking with Him frankly and plainly, asking His assistance in all his affairs, just as they occurred. God never failed to respond.

He was also guarded by the Holy Spirit. During his 15 years in the monastery kitchen, he was never bored. He found everything he did to be easy because he did all of it for the love of God.

It is impossible not only that God should deceive, but also that He should long let a soul suffer which is perfectly resigned to Him, and resolved to endure everything for His sake.[1]

Brother Lawrence believed that many human ills would disappear if we turned to God, focused on Him and practiced His presence. Did he find it easy to do? Not at first It took time to develop the habit, but he had his entire life to do so. He believed that a relationship with God and the practice of His presence came down to three things:

Faith. All things are possible to those who believe. Hope. All things are less difficult when you hope. Love. Life is easy for those who love, and still easier for those who persevere in the practice of these three virtues.[2]

I wrote down some advice from one of Brother Lawrence's letters to encourage us as we grow older—and as we grow in grace, gratitude and grit:

Pray remember what I have recommended to you, which is, to think often on God, by day, by night, in your business, and even in your diversions. He is always near you and with you; leave him not alone. You would think it rude to leave a friend alone who came to visit you. Why, then must God be neglected?[3]

And finally, here is one of his prayers to inspire you:

O my God, since Thou art with me, and I must now, in obedience to Thy commands, apply my mind to those outward things, I beseech Thee to grant me the grace to continue in Thy presence and to this end do Thou prosper me with Thy assistance, receive all my works and possess all my affections.[4]

GRACE

I will give thanks to the LORD because of his righteousness and will sing praise to the name of the LORD Most High.

(Psalm 7:17)

GRATITUDE

Lord, thank You for the example of Brother Lawrence.

GRIT

Today, I will practice the presence of God, and when my attention wanders, I will confess my humanness and trust God to bring me back into His presence.

Notes

1. Brother Lawrence, *The Practice of the Presence of God* (Nashville, TN: Thomas Nelson Publishers, 1999), p. 7.
2. Ibid., p. 10.
3. Ibid., p. 29.
4. Ibid., p. 12.

Just Enough Light

I'm fed up and burned out. I've just plain had it!" I said to a friend over the phone one morning after waking up feeling overwhelmed.

"What you need is a day in the mountains," my friend said. "Remember last year when . . ."

I remembered well the event she referred to. An important decision about my life direction was looming. I needed time alone to think and pray. I had always found God's voice to be especially clear when I walked in the woods, so I drove out to Morena Park, about an hour outside San Diego, and pulled into the campsite with an expectant heart.

"Lord," I said in prayer while walking that afternoon, "please speak to me. Shed Your light on my path—on my writing, on my home and family, on my church work. I feel in the dark about what to do next." I took a deep breath and tried to relax, surrendering to His time frame.

That evening, after a bit of conversation around the campfire with others, I excused myself early and started down the path to my tent some distance away. I had deliberately chosen a spot where I would have privacy and peace. A sudden chill came over me, however, as I realized how dark it was on the road and how inadequate my small flashlight was. I had only enough light to cover one footstep at a time.

"Lord, I'm scared," I suddenly cried, my voice shaking as I walked between a large grove of towering pines with-

Getting Personal
with Scripture

There's a popular cliché that says: "When the going gets tough, the tough go shopping." *Tee hee!* I think. How much better it would be, however, if during such times the tough went to the Bible. It doesn't get any better than this:

> Be strong and courageous. Do not be afraid or terrified because of them, for the LORD your God goes with you; he will never leave you nor forsake you (Deut. 31:6).

> God is our refuge and strength, an ever-present help in trouble (Psalm 46:1).

> When you pass through the waters, I will be with you; and when you pass through the rivers, they will not sweep over you. When you walk through the fire, you will not be burned; the flames will not set you ablaze (Isa. 43:2).

> Peace I leave with you; my peace I give you. I do not give to you as the world gives. Do not let your hearts be troubled and do not be afraid (John 14:27).

God speaks to us in such personal and reassuring ways. Our opportunity, then, is to receive His comfort and to make it ours. One way to do that is to write out one or two of our favorite verses each day or once a week, inserting our name in pertinent places, so that we can experience God's words for ourselves and our situation. Here are a few examples:

> Peace I leave with you, *Karen*; my peace I give you. I do not give to you as the world gives. Do not let your hearts *(your heart, Karen, and those of your loved ones)* be troubled and do not be afraid (John 14:27).

> *Gene*, God is our refuge and strength, an ever-present help in trouble (Psalm 46:1).

> When you pass through the waters, *Joanne*, I will be with you (Isa. 43:2).

Another way to make the Word of God personal to you is to write out a verse, phrase by phrase, and then amplify it as it applies to your life. Here's an example using Deuteronomy 31:6:

> *Be strong and courageous.*
> Turn away from weakness, Karen. Shore up your mind and body. Take on the authority that is yours in Christ Jesus to do difficult things and succeed.

> *Do not be afraid or terrified because of them*
> Karen, give up fear and worry. Let go of intimidation and terrified feelings based on what someone else does or doesn't do.

For the LORD your God goes with you;
What can man or woman do to you, Karen, when you're walking with God and He is walking with you? When a person *goes with* another, it means he or she is steadfast at one's side, never wavering. That's what God does. He is with you, Karen, always.

He will never leave you nor forsake you.
Never. What a huge word. That means there won't be even one moment, Karen, when God is not with you in every way and in every place. And He promises never to forsake you. Imagine that—you, Karen, are safe no matter what occurs and no matter who rises up against you.

The next time the going gets tough, skip the mall. Turn to the Bible instead and get personal with Scripture.

GRACE

And we also thank God continually because, when you received the word of God, which you heard from us, you accepted it not as the word of men, but as it actually is, the word of God, which is at work in you who believe.
(1 Thessalonians 2:13)

GRATITUDE

*Lord, thank You for Your Word that is sharper than
a two-edged sword. May it go deep in my heart so that
I will apply it to my life each day.*

GRIT

Today, I will choose a favorite verse of Scripture and personalize it and meditate on it, especially when the going gets tough.

Section 2

FAMILY

*BELIEVE IN THE LORD JESUS, AND YOU WILL BE
SAVED—YOU AND YOUR HOUSEHOLD.*
ACTS 16:31

There are moms, dads, sisters, brothers, grandmas and
grandpas, aunts, uncles, and cousins. And there are "steps"
too, if your parents or you as an adult divorce and remarry.
Family! We love 'em. We hate 'em. We laugh with them.
We cry over them. We run to them. We run from them. But
most of us can't get along without them—
even when there has been pain and
hurt. Being family includes love
and forgiveness, joy and acceptance. "These are my people,
and they're wonderful,"

one woman said with a catch in her voice as she reflected on her extended family. "I'm just beginning to get that at age 35."

As a child, I remember that I used to love to spend the weekend at my cousin Pat's house. She lived in a great old house in Chicago, Illinois. It had two attic rooms with slanted ceilings. I loved sleeping in that cozy little space and waking up to the sound of tree branches brushing against the window pane and the fragrance of pancakes on the griddle in Aunt Janet's kitchen.

I also recall dreading to have to kiss Aunt Bernice. A bristly hair stuck out of a mole on her cheek and poked me whenever I came in contact with it. I shivered and jumped back every time! But she too was one of "my people," and I loved her.

Sir John Bowring, nineteenth-century British ambassador, put it elegantly: "A happy family is but an earlier heaven." The writings in this section may bring up a variety of memories about "your people" to savor or to shun—but also to embrace as part of your life.

Fagedda-bout-it!

I recently caught a snippet of an old movie while channel surfing. I didn't stay with it long enough to get the title, but I do remember one line, and it has remained with me. A tough-guy character from Brooklyn—you know the kind, cigarette hanging from his mouth, greasy hair slicked back and a tattoo plastered on his right arm—looked another tough guy in the face, grabbed his shirt with an angry fist and raged, "Fagedda-bout-it! You're making yourself sick. You hear?"

I shuddered at his tone and then flipped to another channel. But the warning, "Fagedda-bout-it," thundered in my mind. Forget the pain of divorce. Forget the abuse at a mother's hands. Forget the sting of a brother's betrayal.

However one expresses it, the demand is the same: Drop it! And then comes the hot poker to the heart: "You're making yourself sick." Someone has the nerve to tell you that *you* are making yourself sick when someone else was the perpetrator.

I've always wondered if anyone really can forget rejection, abuse and betrayal. The thing done to us is in our minds. It doesn't just go away. So what's the point of telling someone to fagedda-bout-it, that holding on to it is making him or her sick, that going over the details is hurting him or her more than the one who caused the pain in the first place?

The point is, it's true. We make ourselves sick when we hold on to memories of hateful acts and those who caused them, especially those to whom we are related. When it comes to family, we need them, and no matter how much pain and disappointment we've suffered at their hands, forgiveness is the only route to healing and wholeness. This is especially true in our older years. We don't know how much time we have left, so making what's left count for good becomes all important.

I remember Pastor Mark (the pastor of the church I attend) saying one Sunday morning when I most needed to hear it, "Every future has a past, and whether we like it or not, God has given us the past as a gift to keep us oriented to our future." When we close the door on the past, we hurt ourselves and everyone we love.

Pastor Mark reminded us, however, that if we allow it, the past can be our guide to present understanding and future behavior. It can also be our friend if we:

- remember that Christ died for our sins, as well as the sins committed against us;
- repent of the choices we made that we didn't have to make; and
- receive God's tender mercy through Jesus Christ.

We can then enter the process of becoming holy and being made clean. And then we can begin praying for those who persecuted us (see Matt. 5:44) and for those we have persecuted by our hateful thoughts.

I have found that it's almost impossible to hold a grudge against someone and pray for him or her at the same time—especially if that person is a mother or father or an adult child, sister or brother!

For years, Maureen's hatred was directed toward her father. She couldn't bear to think about how much she had suffered because of him. "He never wanted me in the first place," said Maureen, now in her 60s. "He wanted a boy to help him in his landscaping business. He tolerated me at best. All I ever wanted was to hear him say, 'I love you.' But I never did while growing up."

When Maureen's father was dying years later, she went to visit him. By that time, her mother had passed away, and he was alone. Maureen said that she went out of respect ("Honor your father and mother . . ."), nothing more. She was surprised by what God revealed when she walked into her father's hospital room.

"I looked at the person in the bed—my father—a lonely, broken, frail, very old man with parched skin, withered hands and watery eyes. No longer was he the hulk I remembered, the one who could frighten me to the core with just a word or a look. He no longer had any power over me."

Maureen took her father's hands in hers and said, "Daddy, I love you. Can you forgive me for not being the child you wanted?" Her father nodded and began crying softly. He squeezed her hand and pulled her close. "Then I told him that he had never been the father I needed," said Maureen, "but I forgave him."

Maureen had only a few hours with her dad, but she said those hours were precious. "I was healed that day," she said. "It was as if Jesus had replaced my heart with His. I actually felt love for my father."

To hang on to hurt, anger and revenge is to inflict more pain on yourself than you received in the first place. The wound festers and enlarges until it consumes your mind and heart. You become the victim of the wrongdoing all over again—only this time to a greater degree. To forgive another is to love and free yourself. And if the other person is set free in the process, so be it. He or she is still responsible before God for the action taken against you.

We forgive others because Christ first forgave us. "Be kind and compassionate to one another, forgiving each other, just as in Christ God forgave you" (Eph. 4:32). If ever you have a problem forgiving one of your family members, ask the Lord to expose your heart and to bring to light any ways in which you have contributed to the brokenness. You may have been blinded to your part in the problem, and that has kept you from giving and receiving forgiveness.

Consider what Christian author Lawana Blackwell once said: "The hatred you're carrying is a live coal in your heart—far more damaging to yourself than to them." Forgiving is a decision, not a feeling. It can be freeing to know that although our emotions may fluctuate from day to day, our commitment to forgiveness will keep us moving forward.

If you are sincere in your desire to restore and rejoice in your family relationships and to make the most of the time you have left with one another, you will not waste it trying to reconstruct former conversations, explain your position, set the record straight, accuse and counteraccuse, or assign responsibility for who said what to whom when and where. Instead, you will be eager to let go of emotional baggage, blame, shame and the need to be right. You will find yourself more than ready to faggeda-bout-it, to focus on healing the wound, leaving the rest to the Lord, where it belongs.

GRACE

For if you forgive men when they sin against you,
your heavenly Father will also forgive you.
(Matthew 6:14)

GRATITUDE

Dear God, I am grateful for the gift of family.
Help me to love them as You do, regardless of
what has happened in the past.

GRIT

Today, I will do something specific (a favor,
a surprise, a helpful action, a word of encouragement or thanks) to show my family that
I love and appreciate them.

The Green Coat

Pearl S. Buck, novelist and speaker, won the Nobel Prize for Literature in 1938, the year I was born. I had never heard of her until I was in high school and her prize-winning novel, *The Good Earth*, was required reading in an English class. That assignment led me to read about her life and eventually to write about her in one of my books for young adults.

A moment in her life that stood out for me occurred just 11 years before she received the Nobel Prize. While living in Nanjing, China, with her husband, John, an agricultural teacher, and their two daughters, Pearl wrote her first novel in the attic room of their modest home. She finished the book early in 1927 but never had a chance to submit it for publication. In the spring of that year, a great uprising against China's warlords took place. This revolt was carried out by a combined force of soldiers loyal to China's two major political parties, the Nationalists and the Communists.

The revolutionary armies invaded Nanjing on March 27, intending to take over the city. As the troops advanced, the Bucks were forced to flee from their home. A servant whom Pearl had helped many times before allowed the family to hide in her small mud hut. Later that evening, they were discovered by the invading soldiers, who took the Bucks to a university where other Caucasian prisoners were being held. For a time, Pearl thought that everyone was going to die. Finally, the Chinese generals agreed to release the non-Chinese prisoners, and they allowed the Bucks to board an American destroyer.

The Bucks arrived in Shanghai with no more than the clothes on their backs. The invading soldiers had destroyed Pearl's recently finished novel, and looters had taken her books and her beautiful green coat. Yet Pearl claimed that she felt a sudden sense of freedom, despite the great loss. "I knew now," she later wrote, "that anything material can be destroyed. On the other hand, people were more than ever important and human relationships more valuable."[1]

I once owned a green coat—when I was about 13. I can still picture its wide collar, shiny buttons and smart belt, which I loved to cinch tight around my small waist. My mother bought me a hat to match, and I felt like a fashion princess whenever I wore this outfit.

Within a year or two, I had outgrown the coat and hat and gave them away. I didn't think of my coat again until I read about Pearl's and the fact that someone had taken it from her before she was ready to give it up. An experience like that feels like an invasion, and the sense of loss can be greater than if one had voluntarily given up the item. I wondered how I'd have felt if someone snatched my green coat when it meant the world to me.

Today, however, as an older woman who has had many coats and hats and dresses and shoes in my life, I am not as attached to any one belonging—or any one place, for that matter. Of course, I'm aware that the loss of something precious in the material world can't compare to the loss of a family member through death or divorce. There will always be another green coat but never another mother or father or child or brother or sister.

I see this more clearly as my husband and I sort and toss and give away things before moving to our new city.

As I pile clothing into bags, I'm reminded of the day I bought a certain sweater or scarf or a piece of jewelry. I can see myself in the fitting room being so excited about a particular item—an item that within a few years or less would be ready for the discard pile.

Not so with the people in my life. I treasure every moment with my children and grandchildren, sisters and brothers and their families. Petty concerns and annoying differences between us have melted like a marshmallow in hot chocolate. I remember only the sweetness and the warmth of being together.

My favorite chair, a special book, a lovely pen or a cozy blanket cannot compare to the lilt of a grandchild's laughter, the love that shines from my son's eyes, the playful smile that is unmistakably my daughter Julie's, the attentive look I receive from my daughter Erin when I need to talk.

As I age, I want to be quick to smile, to listen, to be available and to give to my family with a generous heart—whether money, time, service, a listening ear or a green coat.

GRACE
Just as I gave you the green plants, I now give you everything.
(Genesis 9:3)

GRATITUDE
Dear God, thank You for things to play and work with,
food to eat and clothing to wear—for all the material
goods You have provided for me to enjoy while I am here.

GRIT
Today, I will look at my possessions, and I will give to
someone in my family something dear to me as a
reminder that people are more important than things.

Note

1. Pearl S. Buck, quoted in Karen O'Connor, *Contributions of Women: Literature* (Minneapolis, MN: Dillon Press, 1984), p. 62.

Totally Tickled

I remember reading a newspaper article titled, "Totally Ticked Off." The author suggested that people are cranky because of unrealistic expectations at home, at work, or in the neighborhood. It doesn't take much to set us off, especially as we grow older. If we run into an impatient clerk at the grocery story, an indifferent teller at the bank, a fast-food server in slow motion (particularly when we're starved and still have an hour's drive home), we are ready to draw, aim, fire!

Then there are the people we love, the ones we refer to as family. We invite a daughter or son to dinner, and he or she forgets or shows up late or comments on the vegetables ("Mom, you know I hate lima beans!"). Maybe your spouse shows a wrinkled brow every time you forget to put the carton of milk on the top shelf of the fridge, where it's easy to see. Or perhaps your own mother treats you like a 10-year-old in front of your best friend, talking about you as though you're not at the same table in the same restaurant as she is.

When my husband and I bought our first home together at age 55 and 65, my father, then 85, sounded *ticked* instead of *tickled*. He did not congratulate us. He worried aloud that we wouldn't be able to make the mortgage payments.

It was then I realized the importance of being tickled instead of ticked. How is this possible, though, when there are so many people in the world, including those in our families, who seem determined to irritate us? It's possible through this simple action: Decide to be tickled, regardless of the situation or circumstances. Don't let anyone rob you of your contentment. Instead of succumbing to other people's agendas, set your own. See yourself as a blessing and then *be* one.

If you disapprove of a choice or decision, keep silent unless asked for your opinion (unless there's abuse or violence involved, but I'm not talking here about extremes, just the normal day-to-day ebb and flow of family life).

Being ticked alienates and divides. Being tickled encourages and nurtures. Decide now never to allow time pressure, information overload or unrealistic expectations get in the way of you standing *with* your family members, blessing them in prayer, offering help when needed and loving them without conditions.

So the next time your son announces he's moving to another state (and taking your daughter-in-law and grandchildren with him) or your spouse says he's going to learn the guitar at age 68 or start a small business or plant tomatoes, close your eyes and ears to the negative comments waiting to spill forth and instead say five simple words: "I'm totally tickled for you"—and mean them.

GRACE
Shout for joy to the LORD, all the earth.
(Psalm 100:1)

GRATITUDE
Dear God, please help me to be tickled instead of ticked,
to be a blessing instead of a burden.

GRIT
Today, I will show my family in a tangible way,
such as a note, a telephone call, an e-mail or a hug,
that I am tickled about them and for them.

Being a *Great* Grandparent!

Tucked away in the minds of many people today is a loving memory (or fantasy) of a grandmother in a flower-print apron busily preparing a multicourse Thanksgiving dinner or whipping up a batch of chocolate chip cookies, eager to enfold her grandchildren in her full, soft arms at any time of the day or night. Grandpa, on the other hand, is a friendly handyman who can fix a bike in a flash, tell a yarn a mile long about the old days, milk a cow and bounce a crying baby on his knee.

Some grandparents today still fit that picture—and blessed are those grandchildren who have access to them. But what about grandmothers who can't, don't want to or no longer bake? Or grandfathers who can't pound a nail straight, have never seen a cow face-to-face or are nervous around babies under six months old?

Can they too be upstanding members of the Grandparents' Club? Yes! There's room for all of us, despite our differences. Grandparents, just like grandchildren, come in different shapes and sizes and personality types, and each of us has something unique to bring to the relationship.

What is special about you as a grandparent? What do you most like? What, if anything, do you dislike? Sometimes a better understanding of ourselves can help us slip into our relationship with our grandchildren—and their parents—as comfortably as we would a cozy pair of house slippers.

One of the most important things we can do to be a *great* grandparent is to express our true selves. Stereotypes are out. Individuals are in. That's good news for those of us who are still actively working in our careers, traveling, volunteering, going back to school, or taking up a new and exciting hobby. One grandmother I heard of is taking flying lessons. A grandfather has gone back to college to get his degree. Another woman opened her own needlepoint shop. She decided to turn a hobby into a profit-making venture. Others are enjoying freedom from work and look forward to more leisure time with family and friends.

You can also be a *great* grandparent no matter what kind of a dwelling you live in: a trailer or tent, a condo or cottage, a hotel or a house. It's who you are that matters to the grandkids, not where you live or how many material goods you give them. The really important things haven't changed, namely your presence in the life of your grandchildren exactly the way you are. You may not bake cookies, but if you can play tag or climb a tree or hang out at the park or read a story or braid hair or rustle up a homemade pizza, you'll find some takers!

Let your grandchildren and their parents know what you can and want to do and what you're available for. And tell them what you're not open to. More relationships are spoiled because of unrealistic expectations than because of any other reason. It's okay to have a life of your own—a life that includes your grandchildren and their parents as well as other people and activities that matter to you.

More often than not, grandchildren want a listening ear, a warm snuggle, a pat on the shoulder, a word of encouragement. And these are things every grandparent can give.

Grandparents who I think of as truly great are those who experience joy—both in their relationship with their grandkids and in life in general. They have enough turf underfoot by the time they've reached the half-century mark that nothing gets in the way of living a joy-filled life moment by moment. They're excited to wake up in the morning, to breathe, to walk and talk with friends and family, and to praise God for the riches they have even in the smallest corners of their lives: a flower or two poking out of a bed of weeds in the yard, a steaming cup of tea and a blueberry muffin across the table from someone they love, the dependability of a good friend who has seen them through a crisis.

Children notice our moods and our methods. If we are full of joy, our grandkids will pick it up and incorporate it into their lives. And what about exploring a new dimension of life? "I never thought I'd roller-skate again," said Grammy Louise. "I hung up my skates a long time ago. But when my grandson asked for Rollerblades for his eighth birthday, I thought, *Why not buy two pairs, one for him and one for me?* You should see the two of us. We have a fine time rolling down the sidewalk at the park."

I had a similar experience with my grandson Noah. We both love to hike and climb. When he was a youngster, the mountains and the desert were our special places. After a youth outing in the Mojave Desert, I asked him what his favorite memory was. "You and me hiking together," he said. Those words filled me up for days.

I've discovered that I'm a *great* grandma when I'm doing with my grandchildren what I do for myself—trying something new, continuing to learn, respecting my limitations as I age, and expressing myself honestly whenever I talk. I have the freedom to say, "I can do this, but not that" and be respected for it.

Many grandparents I've spoken with confided that their grandchildren have opened up for them an entirely new world of experiences, including:

- going down the slippery slide at a water park;
- picking fresh strawberries together and turning them into a pie;
- sleeping in a tent (by someone who claimed she hated camping until her grandson begged her to go);
- learning more about ancestors by helping a teenaged grandchild put together a family scrapbook or album for a social studies project.

The most important aspect of being a *great* grandparent is letting your grandchildren in on your relationship with God. You can weave spiritual themes into playtimes as well as times of prayer. You don't have to make an issue of it. Simply do what seems natural in the moment.

I became a Christian later in life, so I don't have as much to share about my early childhood experiences with God as someone who grew up knowing the Lord might have. But that's okay, too. It's part of who I am. I tell my grandchildren how blessed they are to know the Lord at such a young age. Now they'll have a best friend within their heart for the rest of their lives. And of course, you can use story times to add to their knowledge of how God works in the lives of His people—from Adam and Eve right down to their own lives.

When you build a foundation of spiritual connection with your grandchildren, it will be there in times of crisis and need. Many teenagers and young adults I've spoken with have acknowledged their grandmother or grandfather as a source of spiritual truth, nurture and stability in their lives. What a legacy! No savings bond, vacation or new toy or trinket can take the place of such a gift.

GRACE
Do not forget the things your eyes have seen or let
them slip from your heart as long as you live.
Teach them to your children and
to their children after them.
(Deuteronomy 4:9)

GRATITUDE
*Dear God, I am grateful for the gift of grandchildren.
They are apples of gold in my life.*

GRIT
Today, I will do something unexpected, even risky,
with one or more of my grandchildren—something
that will challenge and bless us.

Next Best Thing

I can't keep up with all the invitations and celebrations," commented one woman of 70-plus years. "I don't have the energy I used to have."

A man 10 years older heard us talking over a taco at a local eatery. He looked surprised. To him, the parties and dinners and family get-togethers are what keep him alive. "Never say no to an invitation. That's my motto," he said with a nod of his head.

So what's an aging body to do (besides saying a flat no) if you find it a challenge to continue attending family functions as you grow older? Well, here's another opportunity to ask for grace, express gratitude and take action with a bit of grit!

Before you turn down an invitation, think it through. Are you simply in the habit of saying "I can't make it" when you really could? You might ask someone to drive you. Or you could plan ahead by taking a nap the day of the event so that you'll have the energy needed to join in the festivities.

You might also consider how important your presence is to the people involved. It can be a greater gift than anything you could purchase. On the other hand, there are times when you simply can't make it. You would if you could, but you have a conflict, or you'll be out of town, or you're ill. That's life—and we all have those days when no matter how interested we are, we simply cannot get to the event. What then? Are we all washed up? Out of chances? Blacklisted for good?

Not if you make a point of doing the next best thing. Bestow your presence in a slightly different way. In so doing, you'll still be offering your love and support every bit as much as if you were there in person.

First, be willing to go out of your way. Think about something you could do that would show your family that you care. Suppose you're in Hawaii the same week your daughter-in-law is performing in a community play. Send a bouquet of flowers with a personal note. That will certainly get her attention and show her that you're thinking of her and wishing her well, even though you can't be there in person.

Suppose your grandson is in the playoffs for the high school basketball team but you live 2,000 miles away and you don't travel as easily as you once did. Call and pray with him before the game. Send a box of candy to share with the team. Find out some interesting facts about a few of the players and be ready to weave them into a phone conversation. What teen wouldn't be blessed and impressed with a grandparent who was "up" on things that mattered to him or her?

What about an event you totally forgot about? You had said yes, and then you blew it! You woke up to the fact after it was too late. Do you ignore the faux pas or do you fess up and take your lumps?

I vote for fessing up. It's cleaner that way and it shows humility—a virtue often in short supply among older people in our culture. When you miss an event because of a mess-up, it's time to make amends. Say, "I'm sorry." Ask for forgiveness. Find a way to make up for the blooper. Set a date for lunch or a movie or a long walk. Above all, don't let guilt compound your absence. If you didn't make the event—whether a birthday party or football play-offs—go to the person (in person, if possible) and apologize.

It's okay to be human. In fact, we don't have a choice. We all make mistakes, regardless of age. The problem grows, however, when we ignore it, gloss over it, and hope it will go away. It doesn't, and it won't. It gets bigger, and then the amends take longer and require more energy. That puts you back where you started—too tired or too old to say yes in the first place!

Stop the cycle now. Be there whenever you can. And when you can't, do the next best thing.

GRACE
For if you forgive men when they sin against you,
your heavenly Father will also forgive you.
(Matthew 6:14)

GRATITUDE
Dear God, I am grateful that my family wants my company and includes me in all their celebrations.

GRIT
Today, I will practice saying yes, but if I must say
no sometimes, I will show my interest with a
phone call, a special gift, a letter or a card that
adds my spirit to the occasion.

What Adult Children *Really* Need

"Mom, I'm losing it," Jeannie told her mother—my friend Sue—over the phone in a moment of panic. "Being a mom is hard. Why didn't you tell me?"

They both chuckled, even though Sue knew that her daughter meant what she said. Sue had seen signs of stress the last few times they were together. Jeannie had been short with her son and daughter and overwhelmed with the needs of a colicky baby.

Sue offered to make the three-hour trip to Jeannie's house and spend a few days to help her get through the storm. She remembered such a time in her own life when all she needed was "Mom," and her own mother flew to her side.

I recall a similar occasion with my youngest daughter, who was also a mother of three young children. I lived too far away to come to her rescue at the moment, but I did offer to pray with her over the phone each day. It made all the difference. Another time, my son called, breathless and troubled. He *had* to speak to someone. I was glad he chose me. We talked for a couple of hours. I prayed for him, and he hung up feeling calm and grateful. And so did I.

My children are now in their 30s and 40s. For a time, I thought my parenting duties were over. I had slipped comfortably into the role of a friend—until the events in my friend Sue's life arose and reminded me that I will never be as much a friend to my children as a parent. They no longer need me to clothe, feed and house them, but they still need me to love, nurture and support them. So, my parenting continues—and I'm happy it does, for I love being a mother.

Whether your adult children live around the corner, up the block, across town or miles away, they will always be your "kids" and the urge to parent them will always be there. To make my relationship with my children the best possible, I find it helpful to consider what my son and daughters *really* need. Here's what I came up with. Perhaps my observations will inspire you to look at what your adult children want and need from *you*.

Sensitivity

Pay attention to what's going on. Check out the surroundings and the emotional climate when you're with your son or daughter. Some parents barge into their children's home and take over. One mother I heard about arrived unannounced one evening and then was hurt when she wasn't welcomed with open arms. She didn't understand. She simply wanted to lighten her children's load with a home-cooked meal. She meant well, but her timing was off. The family was getting ready to entertain houseguests from out of town. They weren't prepared for an unexpected visitor—even if it was mom or grandma.

I remember my own mother complaining about her father. He made light of issues that were serious in her mind. He just laughed her off when she confided in him, saying, "You make too much of small things. It will all work out." She was hurt by his lack of sensitivity to the things that worried her. What she needed was loving encouragement, not dismissal.

Solace

My daughter Erin called one day to share the news that her best friend had just lost the infant son she had anticipated for nine months. The child was stillborn. It would have been easy to divert Erin's grief with a story of my own, or a comparison to another family, or a platitude that I might have thought would bring comfort. Fortunately, I knew better *this* time because I had learned from previous experiences. All Erin really needed from me was a listening ear, a comforting prayer, and a willingness to simply understand her deep feelings.

I knew that I had struck the right note when Erin said at the end of our conversation, "Thanks for listening." I wondered why it had taken me so long to realize that I could accomplish more good as a mother by standing *with* my child than by trying to change her position because I was uncomfortable with it.

Support

Braces. Singing lessons. Gymnastics. Football. Summer camp. The needs of our grandchildren can overwhelm their parents, especially those parents who are still building their careers or are already sacrificing time, money and energy for one parent to remain at home as their children are growing up.

This is perhaps one of the most important seasons in their lives as a family and in our lives as the parents of adult children. Our sons and daughters crave our support, even if they don't readily admit it. They may be trying to prove their independence as well as their ability to make wise choices. Let them, but be available to help pick them up when they fall— to help with financial gifts when it is the right thing to do.

I've told my kids that I won't pay their household bills, but that I do want to contribute to extras for the grand-children, such as music lessons, camp or a school field trip. It's easy to go overboard, as older parents generally have more income to spare than their adult children.

We can overstep our boundaries if we appear to take over or put down our children's ability to provide for their families. My own father had this tendency when I was a young mom. I appreciated the help he provided, but I often felt obligated to him after I accepted the money. When it comes to *support*, it is crucial for us to respect our adult children and to ask permission before we step in and pay for things that may not sit well with them.

To me, the most important form of support is prayer. Our children can trust us to stand in the gap for them, holding them up to the Lord each day for His protection, guidance and wisdom.

Serenity

Serenity is a state of calm, of peace, of a deep inner knowing that all is well. This is the plane of life that most of us want to live on. Thankfully, serenity is not tied to any one prac-tice. It is, rather, a spiritual discipline that brings about a state of total well-being as we come to rest in God. To be serene is to be accepting—to hold life, self and other people with an open hand instead of a clenched fist. What a gift this can be to our adult children.

Parents who practice serenity know that their personal power is limited and that they are effective only to the extent that God empowers them. They do not waste time trying to figure out what to do, what to say, or how to respond. They go to God *first* and ask for the power they need to accept whatever comes at them that they cannot change. Then they pray for the courage to change what they can. This takes some doing, because it implies that they will be given that knowledge and that they must then take action.

Finally, and most important, these parents seek the wisdom they need to know the difference between what they can and cannot change. In all situations, they come before God, leaning on His power and understanding, not on their own. In so doing, they release the results to Him, trusting in His just outworking in their lives and in those of their children.

As we take up this spiritual journey, we can turn to these practices with our sons and daughters. Like streams in a desert, we can use these practices to refresh our spirits when we feel dry and to guide us when we feel lost. And for those times when we feel strong and surefooted, these steps will enable us to explore new terrain with the confidence that God is with us every step of the way as loving parents of our adult children.

GRACE
After all, children should not have to save up for
their parents, but parents for their children.
(2 Corinthians 12:14)

GRATITUDE
*Dear God, I thank You for my children. They are
jewels in my crown.*

GRIT
Today, I will give my children at least one thing
that they *really* need instead of giving
what I *think* they need.

Section 3

FRIENDS

*DEAR FRIENDS, LET US LOVE ONE ANOTHER,
FOR LOVE COMES FROM GOD.*
1 JOHN 4:7

Best friends. Casual acquaintances. Sports buddies. Prayer partners. Life is a rich and colorful garden when we have a variety of people to play with, confide in, talk to and share with the ups and downs of each day.

These people become even more precious as we age. Building a history with another person is no small achievement. We don't easily say good-bye to such a man or woman, for as Robert Louis Stevenson recorded in one of his writings, "A friend is a present you give yourself."

I remember my mother-in-law, Ada, weeping over the loss of one friend after another as she moved into her 80s. By age 92, when she died, she was the last one of her circle. I couldn't relate to her heavy heart then because I was much younger and had plenty of people around me. But now, nearly 20 years later, I'm beginning to understand her losses, as some of the men and women I've known are being called home.

While we still have one another, regardless of age, it is important to nurture those relationships with care, loyalty and truth, as the following writings will illustrate.

Love Lines

Jesus ate with friends and strangers alike. He walked among the weary and weak, healing them with His words and His touch. He helped them catch fish. He showed them how to pray. He talked with them as they moved on foot over dusty roads and hillsides.

He didn't hold back because He didn't like the way someone looked or smelled. He didn't judge them by the cloak they wore or the family they came from. He didn't distinguish between men, women and children. All were welcome.

He was the Son of the Most High God, yet to His followers He was a neighbor and friend and a loving, vibrant leader who communicated with them in ways they had never known before. In every situation, He looked to His Father for guidance and did what the Father showed Him. He knew what people really needed and wanted, and He gave more than they could have asked for or dreamed of.

He is a model of friendship for us today, just as He was for the men and women of His time. Jesus was *available*. He spent time with people—in the Temple, on the road, in their homes.

He was *attentive*. Remember His compassion for the daughter of the Roman official? His care for the heartsick sisters after the death of their brother, Lazarus?

He was *aware*. He knew what was going on around Him, and He responded to it. The woman with an issue of blood did not go unnoticed. He felt His power go out to her, and she was healed.

He was *accepting*. He walked among sinners and strangers and embraced them all, just as they were. Mary Magdalene, doubting Thomas, unpredictable Peter—He loved each one.

And Jesus was *appreciative*. He received Mary and Martha's hospitality, and He withdrew to the hillside to pray and to praise and thank His heavenly Father.

As we grow older, being a real friend in a time of need can feel like a chore instead of a privilege. But Jesus shows us how. When it takes time and energy and patience—the very things we may need ourselves or that are hard to come by as we age—we can look to Him for guidance. Part of growing older gracefully is being willing to face tough times and difficult people with grit, and be a friend anyway.

The following are some examples of how to be a real friend—taken from the lives of some people who truly are.

Be Available

According to my husband, Charles, a retired customer-service all-star from Nordstrom, "Being available is what friendship really is about. It takes time to get to know another person. If you're not there, it can't happen."

Charles said he felt more alive and energized in his job when he began putting people ahead of paperwork. Serving customers all day can be taxing. He decided to make it fun by being available on a personal level. He asked questions, joked with the men and women who came to his counter, and opened conversations while he was taking care of their needs. He made friends with strangers, and everyone benefited.

One day, a woman came up to the counter and demanded to see the department manager. Charles leaned forward. "Has someone been beating up on you today?" he asked, playfully. "You seem upset. How can I help?"

The woman was so taken aback, she smiled—perhaps without meaning to! "The minute I reached out to her, she opened up," said Charles. "She apologized for being grumpy and said she didn't need to see the manager after all. She told me that I seemed to know what I was doing! She had just come from kidney dialysis and still felt weak." By the time the woman left the store, Charles said he felt he'd made a new friend.

Be Attentive

Have you ever walked up to someone at an event, and as you talk, the other person nods and makes polite sounds but his or her "presence" is elsewhere? He scans the crowd while he's standing with you. Or she peeks around your shoulder as if to say, "I wonder who else is here." It's chilling to be on the receiving end of such treatment.

We lead such busy lives that many of us have made a habit of doing more than one thing at the same time—even when we're at a party. We talk on our cell phones while driving and cook with one hand while scribbling a list with the other.

Later, we wonder where the years went and why we don't feel as connected to people as we'd like to be. We long for another moment with a friend or neighbor who has died. We're now sure that we would have been more successful at work if we had put people ahead of the profit line.

It's not too late. We can learn from those mistakes. We can change the way we relate to people from this point on. And we're likely to have fewer regrets later on if we do.

Be Aware

A friend of mine had a successful restaurant business for years. He credited it to his weekly round-table meetings with his employees. His wife, Anne, told me once that Frank knew his people would not be effective if they were carrying around emotional baggage. So each Monday morning, he invited them to share whatever they wished—especially those things that might be distracting them. "At the end of the meeting, you could feel the change in the air," said Anne. "Burdens were lifted and people felt closer to one another because they knew some of the challenges others were facing."

Be Accepting

Every one of us can likely point to a time in our lives when we've needed someone in our corner. Someone who would cheer us on, accept us as we are and help us move forward.

Joe, who worked part-time for a stationery supply store doing data entry in the back office, remembers the difference one person made in his life when he started the job. "My first day was agony," he said. "I wanted to bolt. I realized I had so much to learn."

But Joe stayed because of the power of four encouraging words. An older woman who had been the bookkeeper for the company for 25 years brought him a cup of coffee during the morning break.

"She sat down and told me a few stories about her first job, and before long, we were both laughing. She had made every mistake you could imagine."

Joe knew he had a friend and a confidant when she patted him on the shoulder, smiled and with a twinkle in her eye, whispered, "You'll be just fine."

"She accepted me as I was," said Joe. "It was such a relief. Every time I felt overwhelmed, I looked over at Betty and knew that I'd be all right. Because of her example, I've been more accepting and encouraging toward others."

Be Appreciative

Words matter. They have the power to hurt, to heal, to encourage, to console, to bring people together or to tear them apart. They are among the most important means we have of communicating with friends, family, coworkers and neighbors. And two of the words people don't hear often enough are "thank you."

"Thank you for being my daughter."

"Thank you for doing such a great job."

"Thank you for supporting me."

"Thank you for your service."

"Thank you for being a wonderful neighbor."

As the apostle Paul reminds us in 1 Thessalonians 5:18, "Give thanks in all circumstances, for this is God's will for you in Christ Jesus." The more we express gratitude to others, the freer we become of the negative thoughts and emotions that sap our strength and drag us down. Resentment and judgment cannot exist in the same space with appreciation.

"Gratitude is the rosemary of the heart," wrote nineteenth-century author Minna Antrim. How little it would take to sprinkle rosemary into the lives of everyone we meet. A simple "thank you" would do it!

As we are available to and attentive, aware, accepting and appreciative of those around us, we are *living* friendship the way Jesus taught us—with love. "God is love. Whoever lives in love lives in God, and God in him" (1 John 4:16).

GRACE

Now, our God, we give you thanks, and
praise your glorious name.
(1 Chronicles 29:13)

GRATITUDE

*Thank You, Lord, for friends. Most of all, thank You that
You are my friend and that You call me friend.*

GRIT

Today, I will be a friend, as God leads me.

Oxygen for the Soul

Y ou've probably heard the familiar cliché, "If you can't say something nice, don't say anything at all." I'm not sure it applies to every situation. There are times when we have a legitimate complaint or need to speak the truth with words that may hurt—even offend. But there is also a nugget of gold within this saying. When I read it, I'm reminded of the importance of focusing on the nice thing to say, the encouraging word, the uplifting statement.

As people grow older, however, many feel the freedom to set people straight, to offer their opinion or advice (whether or not it's wanted), to pass judgment on another's choices, and to gripe about everything from a pain in the shoulder to poor food at the local deli. How refreshing it would be to take a different path, to focus on praising and encouraging our friends, supporting them as they age and finding ways to make each day better, regardless of the circumstances. Any one of us can do that if we set our mind on it.

Dr. John Maxwell referred to "encouragement" as "oxygen for the soul." In the same way a human being cannot live without oxygen, the soul of a man or woman will shrivel without encouragement. Each of us needs affirming words, sincere praise, an apology when we've been wounded, constructive feedback, a cheerful smile, personal prayer, and more. And we shouldn't have to ask for it or wait to give it to another until he or she is desperate. Today, consider spending more time praising and encouraging your friends, as Jesus invites and commands us to do.

> Each man should give what he has decided in his heart to give, not reluctantly or under compulsion, for God loves a cheerful giver (2 Cor. 9:7).

Are you the life of the party? The leader? The organized one? Or the quiet individual who brings a balanced outlook to every situation? Whatever style comes natural to you, God can use it to encourage others and to bless you as well. Look at your God-given talents. Then decide what you can best give in a cheerful way, neither forcing yourself to do what feels awkward nor measuring yourself against someone else.

> The good man brings good things out of the good stored up in his heart. . . . For out of the overflow of his heart his mouth speaks (Luke 6:45).

"I miss you." "Let's talk." "God loves you, and I do too." "Let's pray together." "Can I help?" Such words of kindness and encouragement are important to all of us. Look at what you need. Then you'll know there are others with the same needs and wants. Get together with those God leads you to and share the caring words you both long to hear. The Holy Spirit will guide, and each of you will walk away uplifted and encouraged.

> Give, and it will be given to you. . . . For with the measure you use, it will be measured to you (Luke 6:38).

A small gift, a loving touch, a drop-in visit. It is amazing how what we give—whether small or great—can bless others with help and hope. And as God promises, as we give, so He will give back to us. What a beautiful remedy for our own needy hearts!

> The effective, fervent prayer of a righteous man avails much (Jas. 5:16, *NKJV*).

My friends and prayer partners Dianna (by phone) and Mona (by e-mail) pray for me and my needs each week. And I do the same for them. They have prayed my children out of trouble, for my husband to find work, and for a new home for us when I thought it would never be a reality. And I have done the same for them over the pressing needs and desires in their lives. We have upheld and encouraged one another for many years. I have not read a book, attended a seminar or heard a sermon that has been more encouraging than Dianna's and Mona's faithful prayers. The prayers of a righteous friend truly avail much more than we can imagine or hope for.

> Let us not become weary in doing good, for at the proper time we will reap a harvest if we do not give up (Gal. 6:9).

Be there when someone needs a friend to lean on, a regret to cry over, a sister or brother in Christ to share with. And when you're in need, the Lord will bring such a person to you. As we commit to encouraging others, God commits to encouraging us by yielding a harvest of friendship, love, support and prayer at just the right time!

GRACE

May the God who gives endurance and
encouragement give you a spirit of unity among
yourselves as you follow Christ Jesus.
(Romans 15:5)

GRATITUDE

*Lord, thank You for giving me oxygen for my soul
so that I might pass it on to others.*

GRIT

Today, I will make a point of encouraging two
of my friends who are in need

Tea and Talk

There's nothing like a lovely cup of hot tea!

Brew a pot of mellow mint when you've had a stressful day. Unload your woes in the company of a dear friend.

Sip a glass of Japanese green tea as you read your devotions and browse the morning newspaper or while chatting with a friend on the phone.

And put on the kettle for sweet apricot tea to accompany a plate of homemade scones. Then call a friend and enjoy the treat as you visit on your sunny patio or warm yourselves in front of a cozy evening fire.

And if you're up late talking and laughing, end the time together with a cup of chamomile, and you'll sleep like an infant.

There is something about tea that opens the heart. I remember many times in my life when its soothing warmth made the way for an unexpected friendship.

In the early '70s, my family moved to a new house. I was bereft at leaving my long-time friends and familiar neighborhood of nearly a decade. But a kind neighbor came to the door one sunny afternoon and welcomed me with a delightful mixture she dubbed Friendship Tea. We became friends that very day.

On another occasion, I met a caring older woman at a women's event at the church I attended. She listened to my sad story about a heartache in my life, and the two of us had a good cry over a cup of hot tea. By the time we dried our eyes, we were ready to smile. Life didn't seem so bad after all. I had someone to talk to, someone who understood and was willing to be with me in that moment of need.

What is this thing called tea, and where did it come from anyway?

The origin of tea is a legend at best, since no one knows its true beginning, but one so believable that perhaps tea came about just as the story goes. In ancient China, Shen Nung, an early emperor and skilled ruler, was a man with an interest in science and the arts and known for his far-sighted edicts. Among these edicts was the command that all drinking water be boiled to protect the hygiene of his people.

The legend states that on a summer day, the emperor and his fellow travelers stopped to rest during a journey to a distant land. His servants immediately drew water and boiled it for drinking. Dried leaves from a nearby bush fell into the hot water and turned it brown in color. The emperor was intrigued by the new liquid, drank some and enjoyed its refreshing taste. And so, according to legend, tea was created.

Today 70 percent of all tea is grown on tea estates in Sri Lanka, India, Indonesia, Kenya, Argentina and China, where the climate is tropical or semitropical. From three basic types—black, oolong, and green—spring more than 3,000 cultivated varieties. As you raise your cup, you're among Americans who drink 140 million cups of tea each day—hot or iced.[1]

Now when I pass down the tea and coffee aisle of my favorite grocery store, I pause and peruse the various labels. Some have elegant names such as Red Zinger, Jasmine Pearls, African Red Bush, and Silver Needle. Others are more practical; you know what you're getting and what they're for: Awake (for the sleepyhead, perhaps?), Calm (for the anxious), Joy (for the one who needs a bit of happiness), and—how about this—Joint Comfort (perfect for our aging "temples," right?).

When it comes to tea and friendship, the following folks speak for us tea-lovers:

There is no trouble so great or grave that cannot be much diminished by a nice cup of tea.

—Bernard-Paul Heroux[2]

Come and share a pot of tea; my home is warm and my friendship's free.

—Emilie Barnes[3]

Strange how a teapot can represent at the same time, the comforts of solitude and the pleasures of company.

—Anonymous[4]

Tea makes a lovely hostess gift, a welcome birthday present or a sweet surprise for any occasion. Why not make some Friendship Tea today and have it ready for that special friend?

Recipe to *Live* For
Friendship Tea

(serves 50)

1 jar (18 oz.) orange-flavored breakfast drink
1 c. sugar
½ c. presweetened lemonade mix
½ c. instant tea
1 box (3 oz.) apricot-flavored gelatin
2½ tsp. ground cinnamon
1 tsp. ground cloves

Combine these dry ingredients and store in an airtight container. Divide into smaller amounts and present as gifts in lovely glass jars. Add a card with the following instructions: "Use 1½ tbsp. per cup of boiling water."

GRACE
He who dwells in the shelter of the Most High
will rest in the shadow of the Almighty.
(Psalm 91:1)

GRATITUDE
*Thank You, Lord, for the gift of a good friend to enjoy over
a lovely cup of delicious tea—both created by Thee!*

GRIT
Today, I will brew a pot of tea and invite a
friend to sit and sip with me.

Notes

1. "The History of Tea," Stash. http://www.stashtea.com/facts.htm (accessed March 16, 2006).
2. Bernard-Paul Heroux, quoted at "Tea Quotes," Tea Rose Lane. http://www.tearoselane.com.au/4512.html (accessed March 16, 2006).
3. Emilie Barnes, quoted at "Tea Quotes," Tea Rose Lane. http://www.tearose lane. com.au/4512.html (accessed March 16, 2006).
4. "Tea Quotes," Tea Rose Lane. http://www.tearoselane.com.au/4512.html (accessed March 16, 2006).

First Things First

W e've outlived all our friends." Grace folded and unfolded her frail, soft hands in her lap and sighed as she shared her sadness. "The older you get, the more important your friends are."

Her words impressed me. I wondered what it would be like to be the last one standing. Most of my friends are still alive, and I enjoy their company whenever I want to. I have friends to walk and pray with and to work and laugh with. And I have friends who absorb my tears when I am down.

As Grace continued, my mind wandered to that ultimate reality. Someday a good friend of mine will die, and I will die one day as well, leaving a friend behind. There is no assurance that my friends will always be there when I need them. And I can't promise that I will always be there for them.

I suddenly felt sad. I put so much stock in friendship. I didn't want to think about a time or place when I would feel alone, as Grace did in that moment. Then God's promise never to leave nor forsake us came to mind (see Deut. 31:6). I became aware again that God is my one true friend and that I am a friend of His.

That led me to consider in a fresh way His great commandment, "'Love the Lord your God with all your heart and with all your soul and with all your strength and with all your mind'; and, 'Love your neighbor as yourself'" (Luke 10:27). If I put first things first—loving and serving God with all my heart and soul—then I will never be alone, regardless of the circumstances. And at the same time, I will be the kind of friend that God wants me to be to those around me—whether the person is my closest buddy, the neighbor next door, or even the stranger down the street.

That last part can be tricky, though. Loving someone as ourselves *sounds* nice, but it's not always easy to practice. What does loving one's neighbor look and feel like in everyday life? Especially when we disagree or misunderstand one another? How can we behave today so that we won't have regrets tomorrow?

"I understand this commandment to mean that relationships come first," says Cori Brown, who is active in prayer ministry at her church and is a technical writer by profession. "As a sinner, I fail constantly, but I'm also yearning to see others with the eyes of Jesus. Sometimes, I become exasperated with erratic drivers, or the behavior of some of my family members makes me crazy, or people at work who complain irritate me. In prayer, however, I can step back and ask my Lord to help me."

For example, the speeding driver might be rushing to a dying mother. The family member may be scared to ask for help. Maybe the person at work had a difficult childhood and doesn't know how to interact with others in a civil way.

But in such moments, Cori thinks about how Jesus would respond to such a person, "I believe He would speak softly, hug him or her and say, 'I love you.'"

Partnership

"I see God and myself in partnership," says June O'Connor, a professor of religion and ethics at the University of California, Riverside. "I depend on God for guidance, strength and support in the hard work and in the joyous experience of loving."

For June, this involves activity and effort, grace and surrender.

"I keep my desire to love alive by studying Scripture, theology and spirituality, as well as through prayers of petition, hope and gratitude and through acts of kindness to friends and strangers," June says. And she seeks to be receptive to God's presence through centering or contemplative prayer, whereby a person receives rather than petitions. As we experience God's comfort and love and wisdom, we're more able to love and nurture our friends through trials and to be happy for them, without envy, in their good times.

Learning Curve

Nancy Reid, Bible study leader and an attorney and mediator who specializes in family law, keeps herself alert to God's commandment by asking herself two questions in her interactions with friends and clients: *Will this action or that decision enhance my faith?* and *Will I be promoting good, loving more, doing God's will?* The answers influence her choice of actions and behavior.

Nancy said she is now at a point in her life where "learning about God" in meaningful ways is making her "more receptive to His leading, more thankful for His good and more loving toward Him and others."

Teaching Love

Ed Piper, full-time teacher in the Juvenile Court and Community Schools of San Diego, California, has spent most of his career in public school classrooms. "In my life," says Ed, "this is the way I love the Lord with all my heart and love my neighbor as myself."

Through daily contact with students, Ed has had the privilege of meeting and working with a wide variety of interesting and challenging individuals such as "young people who are in trouble with the law and adult foreign students" to whom he taught English as a second language.

"Teaching," says Ed, "allows me to take part in these individuals' lives, to share their joys and tragedies. In the context of our relationship, I can then point to the loving God who yearns to know them more."

First things first. Love God. Love others as we love ourselves. This is God's priority. And by God's grace and mercy, it is one we can keep with success—whatever our age—in our relationships with friends, neighbors and everyone we meet.

GRACE

After Job had prayed for his friends, the LORD
made him prosperous again and gave him twice
as much as he had before.
(Job 42:10)

GRATITUDE

*Lord, thank You for the gift of Your Word, reminding me
each day to put first things first and then the rest will follow.*

GRIT

Today, I will make a point of extending a handshake,
a hug, a word of encouragement to my friends and
neighbors and of greeting strangers with the love of
Christ through my thoughts, words and actions.

It Takes All Kinds

Do your friends, like mine, seem at times like pieces in a giant puzzle? Different sizes and shapes that don't easily fit together? A piece of sky is missing here. A flower is absent there. You can't find the right match for the spot of green grass. And where is that last corner that will finish the frame?

> Under His direction the whole body is fitted together perfectly, and each part in its own special way helps the other parts (Eph. 4:16, *TLB*).

So true. As you begin to understand others, you will better understand yourself. What a nice benefit to making friends and becoming a friend to others.

Your friend Mitsy, for example, might be the one full of life and great suggestions for everything from throwing a party to going on a cruise, but she's disorganized when it comes to directing the annual Christmas play at church. If you were in charge, players would arrive on time, costumes and props would be assembled, and the musicians would be tuned up and ready to perform.

A good friend at work is yet another personality type. He'd rather lead than follow. He makes sure employees do things his way. He's not interested in how people feel. He's interested in getting the job done! Yet you do enjoy his company during downtime, because he never misses a beat.

When he makes a promise to meet you for a round of golf, he shows up on time. Your other golfing buddy, however, resists his authoritative tactics. She believes her approach is kinder and friendlier. That puts you in the middle—and it's playing havoc with your stomach.

Maybe another friend runs her home so efficiently that time and money are never wasted. You'd like to be just like her, but it's just not in you to have that much structure.

By understanding the four basic personality types—the Popular Sanguine, the Powerful Choleric, the Perfect Melancholy and the Peaceful Phlegmatic (based on the teachings of Florence Littauer)—you can more easily and quickly bring the pieces of the puzzle, including your own, together into a harmonious whole that will help you understand your own strengths and weaknesses, revitalize your outlook on life, improve relationships at work and develop lasting friendships.

Popular Sanguine

The Popular Sanguine personality is the bright flower of the puzzle. These men and women motivate others to work and play. They are best at making initial contact with people and encouraging and uplifting them, ensuring that the group has a good time—even while working diligently. The Popular Sanguine likes adventure and variety. This person is the one to get involved in planning entertainment for a friendship coffee, welcoming new employees to the workplace, keeping morale up during a church finance committee meeting, or choosing refreshments for a holiday party.

The Popular Sanguine's basic desire is to have fun. Such folks are witty, easygoing, and do not like to be locked into goals.

This describes one of my friends perfectly—and me too, for that matter. Rita and I measure everything by how much or how little fun we'll have. Some people think we're shallow because of it. My friend Diane, for example, reminds me that sometimes one simply has to dig in and do what needs to be done, whether or not it's fun. I see her point. But when that's the case for me, I simply *decide* to make it fun!

Powerful Choleric

The Powerful Choleric personality is the square corner of the puzzle. These individuals prefer to lead than to follow, and they motivate others to take action. They control plans and productivity, giving quick and clear instructions and making sure the group or committee or family sees the immediate gain. Their basic desire is to have control.

Powerful Cholerics come across as bossy and overbearing, however, so don't be surprised if you feel intimidated in their presence (unless you're one yourself!). On the upside, however, Powerful Cholerics provide structure and boundaries for an organization or household. They make outstanding managers, leaders and supervisors at work or in a church body. Sometimes, they are hard to befriend because they are judgmental and can be demanding. I lost a friendship over those very traits. Carol simply could not stay out of my business, and I was making myself sick over her intrusive ways. So, we parted company.

However, many Powerful Cholerics are not that intense. If you're loyal to them, express your appreciation and give them credit for the security they bring to a relationship, they are more likely to trust and share the power. This personality type is also one of the most challenging to warm up to in a new situation. To earn the respect of a Powerful

Choleric, you sometimes have to stand up for yourself—or risk being trampled.

My husband tells the story of a couple of women who came into the shoe department of a store where he worked. Within a moment, he knew who carried the power in the friendship. One woman studied the display, chose a pair of shoes for the other to try on, and then told her to walk the floor to test the fit. The more passive of the two friends walked back and forth for a moment, apparently unsure of herself. Then she looked at her assertive friend and asked, "How do they feel?"

My husband stood there incredulous! Here was a pair of puzzle pieces that fit perfectly, depending on your point of view.

Perfect Melancholy

The Perfect Melancholy personality makes up the straight edges of the puzzle. This is the detail person, the one who keeps the friendship going. He or she arranges get-togethers, remembers birthdays better than anyone and stops by with thoughtful gifts when a friend is ill or out of sorts.

Such men and women are apt to be critical at times and tend toward perfectionism. Their basic desire is to do things perfectly but they are usually accurate and always sincere. Give Perfect Melancholies what they need—order and understanding—and they'll give you what you want. They're good listeners and loyal friends. Look to them for sympathy and understanding when you're down. They care about people and are at their best when needed.

My husband is my best friend on Earth and is a "perfect" Perfect Melancholy. He made the most beautiful scale drawings of the rooms of our new home—complete with movable paper furniture—before we moved in. When the movers delivered our furniture, they simply looked at the drawings and placed each chair and table in the appropriate spot. This paperwork also helped us ahead of time. We were able to sell and donate any pieces we couldn't take with us.

Charles and I are a good fit when it comes to such things. I appreciate such attention to detail—as long as someone else does the attending! And he appreciates my serendipitous response to life.

On the other hand, we clash when it comes to loading the dishwasher or organizing the pantry. The Perfect Melancholy's pantry is "correct." All canned goods of similar category are lined up together. Boxed items have a shelf of their own. Bags of chips and noodles and cookies are contained in a basket on the bottom shelf. The Popular Sanguine's pantry (mine!) holds the same items, but in no special order or sequence. The Popular Sanguine's philosophy is this: As long as the stuff is behind a closed door, that's good enough. Now let's have fun!

Our pantry and dishwasher alternate between Perfect Melancholy and Popular Sanguine, depending on who's in the mood to take on the task. (My husband usually wins because such work is not fun for me!)

Peaceful Phlegmatic

The Peaceful Phlegmatic personality covers the landscape of the puzzle. Such individuals support friends and soothe an upset coworker. They always find a middle ground, even in the midst of chaos. Peaceful Phlegmatics are sometimes indecisive and undisciplined because of their devotion to peace and quiet, but they present a believable and balanced viewpoint that is calming in even the most stressful situations.

However, don't count on the Peaceful Phlegmatic to motivate or rally for a deadline or to organize a neighborhood block party. But he or she is the ideal one to be the friend you need when morale is low.

No matter where you are in the landscape of friendship—from new to long-term—you will begin identifying the personality types around you by observing the way individuals dress, carry out their responsibilities, react to stress, behave during leisure time, and treat you and others. You'll also appreciate the uniqueness and value of each puzzle piece, as well as your own. Then you can live and work, worship and play together effectively and harmoniously "so that the whole body is healthy and growing and full of love" (Eph. 4:16, *TLB*).

GRACE
So in Christ we who are many form one body,
and each member belongs to all the others.
(Romans 12:5)

GRATITUDE
God, I thank You for all the pieces in the puzzle.
They enrich my life as I enrich theirs.

GRIT
Today, I will pay attention to the personality of each
of my friends and look for the gifts in each one.

Friend Ship

Last year, Charles and I went on our first cruise. It was the trip of a lifetime for us. We had always wanted to see the Inland Passage of Alaska, and finally we had the money and the time to do it. I especially enjoyed the fact that everything we needed or wanted from a vacation was right there in one place. To take advantage of what was offered, however, we had to walk to specific locations: a piano bar in one room, a stage show in another, an art auction in still another.

There were also designated areas on the ship for dining, sleeping, reading, playing games, and working out, and two swimming pools, one outdoors and one in. I couldn't get to all of them within a week's time, but that was okay with me, because I knew that this would not be our last cruise. We'd sign up for another and look forward to experiencing a new adventure.

As I started writing about friendship for this chapter, a picture of that large cruise ship came to mind. I envisioned the many friends I have who contribute to me in diverse ways—each one onboard my life, but in different compartments. One brings humor. Another offers wisdom and a listening ear. Some are available for walks or hikes. And still others provide counseling, editing, party advice, dance lessons, decorating help and gardening tips. Many of the same people simply enjoy, as I do, sharing a good time in each other's company.

As I move around my Friend Ship, I see that nearly everything I need and want God has provided through these dear people. Each one is precious to me in his or her own way. I never want to take any one of them for granted or to hold one in higher esteem than another. As we cruise the waters of life, giving and receiving, I'm going to keep in mind the words of Joseph Addison: "Friendship improves happiness, and abates misery, by doubling our joys, and dividing our grief."

I hope these words are true for you, as well.

GRACE
Go in peace, for we have sworn friendship with
each other in the name of the LORD.
(1 Samuel 20:42)

GRATITUDE
*God, I thank You today for my Friend Ship. Each person
who accompanies me on my voyage through life is a special
gift from You for a special purpose.*

GRIT
Today, I will take a closer look at my Friend Ship
and notice how many wonderful people are
onboard to support me in my life. I will call, write
or e-mail a few at a time to let them know I'm
thinking of them.

FOOD

NEVER AGAIN WILL THEY HUNGER; NEVER AGAIN WILL THEY THIRST.
REVELATION 7:16

Food is our common ground, a universal experience," says international chef James A. Beard. It's one of the staples of life we can't live without.

But there are some of us who can't live with it either. We gorge, hoard and surrender to its beguiling fragrances, tastes, textures and comfort. And then we pat our bellies and say, "I'm stuffed. I ate too much—again!"

Becoming comfortable with food appears to be a lifelong journey for

many people as they observe their spreading thighs or pro-
truding fronts. Then, just about the time they stop viewing
food as an enemy, they've gone over the hill and quit caring.
"My taste buds have shut down," one older woman said.
"Finally, I eat to live instead of live to eat. But it's no fun.
I don't enjoy mealtimes like I used to."

A friend of mine recently admitted defeat. "I just can't
cook anymore. I'm bored silly with the whole business."

I feel the opposite way. I've been cooking for more than
40 years, and I still enjoy it. In fact, my husband and I would
rather eat at home than in a restaurant. We've become
attached to our little rituals, made more enjoyable now that
we have updated the kitchen and purchased new cookware.

There is something for everyone in this section, including
"Recipes to Live For." Don't miss them (even if you hate
cooking)!

Down with Diets

Here's my take on an absurd diet I read some time ago.

Breakfast
1 grapefruit or half green apple
1 slice whole-grain toast
1 cup skim or low-fat soy milk

Lunch
1 small piece of lean, steamed chicken
1 cup steamed kale or spinach
1 cup herb tea
1 square of chocolate

Afternoon Tea
Remaining squares of chocolate
1 tub vanilla ice cream with chocolate fudge and whipped cream

Dinner
4 bottles of wine (red or white)
2 loaves of garlic cheese bread
1 super-sized pizza with the works
2 candy bars

Late-Night Snack
1 whole cheesecake (frozen or defrosted)
Raspberry syrup

The reminder at the end brought a good laugh: "The word *stressed* spelled backward is *desserts.*"

This diet is just one of many silly ones that come to our attention via e-mail, the Internet, magazines and books. In a country flowing with dairy, produce, grains, meat, poultry and seafood, I find it humorous that many of us rely on others to tell us what to eat and in what quantities. I have two friends who spent several hundred dollars a week purchasing prepackaged meals from a diet company so that they didn't have to be responsible for their own choices. The company claimed to "take all the work" out of meal-planning and calorie-counting.

And what happened when the program ended? Both friends regained the weight they'd lost. I have a theory about this kind of behavior: When we turn over to others responsibilities that should be ours alone (following God's leading), we don't own the decision to lose weight or to eat properly. There is no personal investment, so there is no satisfying or lasting result.

But when we bring before the Lord our individual needs, our unique challenges and special likes and dislikes, He will lead us. I know this from experience. Diets can and often do mess us up—physically and mentally. Instead of enjoying reasonable portions of a variety of wonderful foods, we label them bad and good, and by extension, we judge ourselves with the same words.

At a dessert and coffee gathering a few weeks ago, a friend watched me take a handful of luscious strawberries instead of the New York cheesecake. "Oh, you're being 'good' tonight," she said. "Well, I'm going to be bad." With that, she heaped a large slice of "sin" on her plate and then smothered it with whipped cream.

"No, I just like strawberries," I responded, "and these look really special."

Enough is enough already! I'm tired of listening to older people punish themselves and then drag a confession out of everyone around them. If you prefer the cheesecake to the berries, go for it. And enjoy each morsel. But don't make me out to be Goody Two-shoes just because I happen to have a weakness for fruit flown in from New Zealand and don't feel a bit guilty about paying $5 a pound for it!

So it's down with diets in my house and up with sensible eating that lifts my heart, satisfies my taste buds and resonates in my spirit. *God is great. God is good. Let us thank Him for this food. Amen.*

GRACE
Then God said, "I give you every seed-bearing plant
on the face of the whole earth and every tree that has
fruit with seed in it. They will be yours for food."
(Genesis 1:29)

GRATITUDE
*I thank You, O Lord, for the great variety of delicious foods
You have prepared for me to enjoy and to share with others.*

GRIT
Today, I will prepare one of my favorite foods
and then sit down and consciously enjoy it without judging the item or myself.

Recipe

To Live For

Miriam's Steamed Fruit Cake

2 c. whole wheat flour
3 tsp. baking powder
1¼ tsp. cinnamon
½ c. raisins or currants
2 Gala or Granny Smith apples, chopped or sliced thin
1 c. cranberries, blueberries or peaches
⅜ c. pure maple syrup
½ c. apple juice

Mix ingredients together. Oil a covered dish lightly and add the mixture. Cover tightly. Place the dish into 1" of water in a large pot. Cover. Steam for 1½ hours.

Serve warm with whipped cream or yogurt.

The Bread of Life

My husband's cousin Harry, a retired minister, loved to share with anyone who'd listen some of the amazing things that occurred as a result of his early morning conversations with God. He started each day with prayer in his favorite chair in the study. "I liked to sit, palms face up, in a gesture of openness," he said. "Then I'd talk a bit, listen a bit, talk a bit and listen some more. Before closing, I thanked the Lord for all His blessings and then asked Him to direct me throughout the day. And He always did."

One Thursday morning, just after Harry finished praying, the word "chicken" popped into his mind. *How strange,* he thought. Harry and his wife, Anne, loved the savory birds they could buy at Redman's Barbecue, but Anne was sick that week and didn't have much of an appetite. Still, the word "chicken" persisted.

"All right, I'll order a few and see where this leads." Harry knew that God was up to something and he was excited to find out what it was.

He reached for the phone to call Redman's Barbecue, where he had placed many orders in the past, when suddenly he remembered that Redman's barbecued chicken only on Tuesdays. This was Thursday. They'd surely be gone by now. But still the urge to call wouldn't go away.

Harry dialed the number, expecting to be told what he already knew. Tuesdays were barbecuing days. However, the cook surprised him. "As a matter of fact," the man reported, "more chickens arrived than usual, so we cooked some today!"

Harry drove right over to Redman's and bought 12 finger-lickin' cooked birds right off the spit. "The number 12 came to me straight from heaven," he said with a chuckle. "I wasn't sure even then what this was all about." Harry put the chickens in his car and began driving. He didn't have a plan. But as he drove, he felt an urge to turn onto this street or into that driveway, sometimes as far away as two miles. "I pulled up to whichever house I was drawn to," said Harry. "Five houses in all."

Harry knew that God had a plan for those chickens, but it was bigger and different from anything he could have imagined. Every person he encountered admitted to praying for food, for money, for provision. Each man and woman was desperate in some way.

"At the first house," said Harry, "a man had just come home from the hospital. He and his wife were in their 80s. She had a heart condition, so she was unable to cook or shop without help." They were in need of food that very day.

"Next I met a woman with three children whose husband had left the family. She had no food and no money. She was really desperate. I left her $20 and two chickens."

At the third house, Harry left a couple of chickens for a man and wife who were ill. The husband was a retired school principal with heart and vision problems, and his wife was sick with the flu.

Harry pulled into another driveway and walked up to the front door. There he met a man who had lost his job just two months before. "I left him a couple of chickens, as well as money for groceries."

The last family needed repairs to their house and didn't have enough food. "They had been too proud to ask for help," said Harry.

"By the time I drove home, I realized that I had no more chickens," he added. "Since Anne was sick, I had offered to cook dinner that night—something simple. When she asked me what we were having, I filled her in on what had happened and then added, 'I planned on barbecued chicken, but they're all gone.'"

Harry did the next best thing. He opened the pantry, looked around, and then turned to Anne and said with a chuckle, "Looks like it's canned stew and saltine crackers!"

While eating, both Harry and Anne had tears in their eyes over how God had used Harry that day. Anne suggested that they stop and give thanks to the Lord. They joined hands and sang the Doxology:

Praise God from whom all blessings flow.
Praise Him all creatures here below.
Praise Him above ye heavenly hosts.
Praise Father, Son and Holy Ghost.

"Then I delivered the last bit of news," Harry said, a wry smile crossing his lips. "I told Anne that the money I had set aside for a movie the next night had gone to the woman with three children who was down to her last dollar."

Anne was all right with that, too. She and Harry dried their eyes, picked up their forks and dug into their canned stew—one of the best meals they had shared in a long time!

You might say that Harry Flowers used a few well-chosen barbecued chickens to share the Bread of Life.

GRACE

Then Jesus declared, "I am the bread of life. He who
comes to me will never go hungry, and he who
believes in me will never be thirsty."
(John 6:35)

GRATITUDE

*Lord, I give You thanks for Your son, Jesus Christ, the Bread
of Life, to all who hear His word and act on it.*

GRIT

Today, I will look for opportunities to share the
Bread of Life with those who hunger and thirst.

Poppin' Good Popovers

(a nice change from bread or dinner rolls)

1 6-c. popover pan
1¼ c. whole wheat flour
¼ tsp. salt
3 large eggs (room temperature)
1¼ c. milk
1 tbsp. unsalted butter, melted
2 tbsp. unsalted butter, cut into 6 even pieces

Oil or spray (with nonstick vegetable oil spray) popover pan.

Preheat oven to 400° F and set rack in middle of oven. Preheat popover pan in oven about 2 minutes. Blend flour, salt, eggs, milk and melted butter by hand or in an electric mixer or food processor for 1 to 2 minutes or until the mixture is the consistency of heavy cream. Use batter at room temperature.

Place one small piece of butter in each cup of popover pan and place back in preheated oven until butter is bubbly, about 1 minute. Fill each cup half full with batter. Bake for 20 minutes. Serve hot with butter, jam or other fruit spreads.

Makes 6 popovers.

Piece of Cake

I remember reading a story some time ago about two sisters who rejoiced with their elderly mother when she called with the news that her recent medical tests had come back "cautiously positive." To celebrate, the three went out for dinner to their favorite Mexican restaurant.

Both sisters had been raised during the Depression and carried with them into their adult lives the practice of eating only half their portions when they dined out and taking the remainder home to be enjoyed the following day. One sister was thrifty as well as calorie-conscious. The other was financially secure but kept an eye on her belt line. And their mother was easily satisfied with a small meal.

So off they went to eat, laugh, talk and give thanks for the good news. Afterward, the sisters said good-bye to their mother and then spent a few moments chatting in the car of the sister who drove. The sister in the passenger seat laid her box of leftovers on the back seat. When they arrived at her house, she waved good-bye and walked inside feeling free of worry and happy with the lovely evening spent with the two women she loved most in the world.

Suddenly, she was ravenously hungry. But as she looked for the carry-out box, she realized that she had left it in her sister's car. Oh no! The enchiladas she had so carefully saved for another time were gone—for good. She laughed out loud at her own foolishness. It was a time to feast, but she had been frugal.

The moral of the story for me as I read it? Sometimes you have to shove all care to the wind—not every day, certainly, but *some* days—and eat and savor and finish every morsel with the ones you love, especially with those who may not be here tomorrow.

Sometimes you just have to eat the whole piece of cake—or in this case, the whole enchilada—and then relish the memory of having lived fully in that moment.

GRACE
Sacrifice fellowship offerings there, eating them and rejoicing in the presence of the LORD your God.
(Deuteronomy 27:7)

GRATITUDE
Lord, I thank You for good news and good food and for feasting and celebrating. I can be frugal some other day.

GRIT
Today, I will invite someone I love to enjoy a wonderful meal with me in a place where we can relax and enjoy one another's company.

"Would you like to have my cake—and eat it too?" I quipped.

"Yes, I would. I was about to ask. Thank you."

She reached over, clutched the plate, swept it out in front of my face and set it down at her place. She devoured every morsel, every crumb, every dab of frosting. I was concerned that she was going to lick the plate clean.

Sandra heaved a sigh of satisfaction and pushed the plate away. Soon the server whisked it off, and that was that. "I'd rather have dessert than dinner anytime," Sandra said.

So I noticed.

Food. We love it. We loathe it. We judge it. We control it. We make up rules about it. We make up lies about it. And we form opinions about people like Sandra, whose eating habits are different from our own.

I'm guilty of all of the above. I've been a student of healthy living for 35 years, and I know a thing or two about food groups and food groupies. I also know a thing or two about soy milk and seaweed, bran and brown rice. And so what!

As I grow older, I'm realizing that I do not need to be the food police for my friends and family. They are more interested in being with me, and me with them, than hearing my latest foray into the world of grains and greens and their impact on digestion and elimination!

And so I am getting it right—finally—in my older years. I am paying more attention to the people I'm with than to the food they're eating. I know what's right for me. I don't know what's right for them. I can leave that to God as well. My life is so much easier when I stop judging and controlling!

I've learned about food and friends from people who clearly have the gift of hospitality, and it has changed me—

and the way I think and behave.

Chuck and Marita Noone of Albuquerque, New Mexico, share spur-of-the-moment dinners with friends and neighbors. "We don't always have an entire evening to spare," says Marita, "but we have enough time to eat together and enjoy some conversation over a simple meal."

Scented candles, pretty napkins, sparkling glasses, intimate lighting and polished silverware can make even the simplest fare seem like a feast.

Some years ago on the other side of the world, I learned another dimension of hospitality. While in Morocco visiting my daughter Julie and my son-in-law who were there on a teaching assignment, I was introduced to the Moroccan custom of afternoon visits. Each day at about 4 o'clock in the afternoon, Julie and I would either call on neighbors and friends or open Julie's home to them. No advanced planning was necessary. It was simply the thing to do.

I returned home wishing that we had such a ritual in the United States. I missed the cozy chats, the warm sweet tea served in small glass containers trimmed in gold, the dainty cookies, a welcome break following a long day. But after a few weeks, I was back to my routine and didn't think about afternoon visits or hot sugared tea again—until sometime later when a friend invited me for lunch for my birthday.

She prepared foods that were new to me: lentil soup, sea vegetables with grated carrot, brown rice and twig tea (yes, twig as in tree)! I went home nourished by her meal, her friendship and her kind gesture, and I recommitted to recovering the lost art of hospitality for myself.

Today, when I think of ways to enjoy the leisure of my older years, I like to choose an action that will nourish both body and spirit. Food is a wonderful means to achieve both. And it doesn't have to take half a day or more to prepare it.

Savory carrot soup and homemade chunky applesauce are two of my favorite dishes. Both are simple, warming and festive. During the winter, especially, I prepare meals that include both. Add steamed rice, hot multigrain bread, herbed green olives and hot tea, and we have a nourishing meal in less than an hour. Invite good friends to join us, and we've created an evening of hospitality and joy-filled moments.

Isn't this part of what it means to grow older gracefully?

GRACE
Everything that lives and moves will be food for you.
(Genesis 9:3)

GRATITUDE
Dear God, I thank You for the abundance of food and drink and spiritual sustenance.

GRIT
Lord, today I will enjoy what You have provided, neither eating nor drinking too much or too little— and I will mind my own business!

Cheri and Jon's "Peachy Keen" Peach Cobbler

2 pkg. frozen pie crusts or homemade pie crusts, enough for a 4-quart glass baking dish
2 tbsp. lemon juice (fresh, if possible)
6 c. peeled, pitted peaches (frozen makes it easier; thaw first)
1¼ c. plus 2 tbsp. granulated sugar
⅛ tsp. salt
¼ tsp. nutmeg
¼ tsp. cinnamon
3 tbsp. flour
4 tbsp. butter

Preheat oven to 450° F. Sprinkle lemon juice over peaches in large bowl. Mix 1¼ cups of the sugar with salt, nutmeg, cinnamon and flour. Add this mixture to the peaches and toss until evenly coated. Line the bottom of a 4-quart glass baking dish with 1 of the pie crusts. (You may have to do a bit of patching if you use round pie crusts.) Spread the peaches on top and dot with butter. Cover the top of the dish with the other pie crust. Flute edges. Cut several vents for steam to escape. Sprinkle the top with the remaining 2 tbsp. of sugar.

Bake for 10 minutes at 450° F. Then reduce heat to 350° F and bake for 30 more minutes. Serve with frozen yogurt, whipped cream, or ice cream. Yum!

Simple Pleasures

Two of my favorite memories from childhood are back-yard potlucks and summer picnics. My parents loved to entertain family and friends, but our small house couldn't hold a large gathering for long, so we would often spill outdoors and carry on our feast at the big wooden table on the grass.

I remember Aunt Janet's potato salad, my mother's apple pie, Dad's grilled hot dogs and burgers, and big juicy watermelons. Of course, we had plenty of lemonade to go around two or three times. I can still taste it.

Family, friends and food just naturally go together, regardless of the seasons of life. I enjoy potlucks and pic-nics as much today as I did more than 50 years ago. Such events bring people together to laugh and talk and relax over a good meal—all the more delicious when the various dishes are the work of many hands.

I like to walk the line first and then go back and sample a small portion of everything offered. Sometimes I even return for seconds, or I approach the person who made a particular treat and ask for the recipe—such as the one I've included at the end of this reading that I've dubbed "Bountiful Bran Muffins." Afterward, it's fun to sink into a comfortable chair and chat with a good friend or favorite relative as you sip an iced tea or hug a cup of hot coffee.

Jesus knew the importance of food and fellowship. He provided for His followers on a hot afternoon in the hills by multiplying fish and bread so that everyone could eat and be satisfied. He often dined with friends, and one of His last events on Earth was a supper with His disciples.

So if you're hankering for some fun and fellowship with others, put together a potluck or a picnic—indoors or out—and invite people to relax with you over a lovely meal—a simple pleasure that will warm your heart as well as nourish your body.

GRACE
You have made known to me the path of life;
you will fill me with joy in your presence, with
eternal pleasures at your right hand.
(Psalm 16:11)

GRATITUDE
*Dear God, I thank You for simple living, for the
delights found on a beautiful buffet.*

GRIT
Today, I will enjoy some simple good things—
a cup of sweet tea, a bowl of fresh fruit and
then a nap in my favorite chair.

Bountiful Bran Muffins

Ingredients List 1

1 egg

2 tbsp. safflower oil

2 tbsp. honey

2 tbsp. molasses

¼ c. plain or vanilla yogurt

Ingredients List 2

1 tsp. baking soda

¼ tsp. sea salt

1 c. wheat bran

¾ c. whole wheat flour

¼ c. water

½ c. blueberries or chopped apples (optional)

Mix together the ingredients in List 1. Mix together ingredients in List 2 and add to ingredients from List 1. Add ½ cup blueberries or chopped apples, if desired. Butter and flour a muffin tin or use paper muffin holders. Bake for 30 minutes at 350° F. Cool before serving with butter or fruit spread.

Soul Food

Is there a soothing comfort food that you turn to when you're feeling lonely, sad, uncertain or even happy and satisfied? Perhaps this food triggers warm memories of the family table and good times with friends and relatives. Such food not only nourishes the body but does the soul a whole lot of good, too.

In the United States, the term "soul food" refers to African-American cuisine, including such mouth-watering delicacies as yams, sorghum, watermelon, pumpkin, okra, leafy greens, wild lemons, oranges, dates and figs. When the aroma of soul food wafts through a neighborhood, everyone knows there's a big pot on the stove somewhere, and they gather 'round.

In my family of origin, there were many delicacies particular to my Irish heritage, beginning with Mom's apple slices (drizzled with a light frosting made from a mixture of water and powdered sugar), corned beef and cabbage (especially on St. Patrick's Day), and plenty of hot stews (with more vegetables than I liked at the time). In my home now, soul food is potato-carrot soup, pumpkin custard and toasted English muffins spread with fresh hummus and topped with thin slices of onion, tomato and avocado.

Musing about the kind of soul food one can eat got me thinking about another kind of "soul food"—the kind that nourishes the human spirit. It is the food that matters for eternity. As we grow older with grace, gratitude and grit, I believe it's important to enjoy earthly foods that keep us healthy, functioning and alert. But such foods should never take the place of a daily helping of true soul food: conversation with God, rest in Him, Scripture reading, journal-writing, listening prayer, and repentance when we overstep God's authority and will for our lives. This rich buffet of nourishing choices provides the balance we all need, especially as we age.

This week as you linger over a cup of tea and your favorite cookie or sit down to a lovely meal, enjoy every bite and sip, keeping in mind that although these will one day pass, the food you feed your soul will—like the words of Jesus—never pass away.

GRACE
Dear friend, I pray that you may enjoy good
health and that all may go well with you, even
as your soul is getting along well.
(3 John 1:2).

GRATITUDE
*God, I thank You today for providing nourishing food for
my body—and more important, food for my soul.*

GRIT
Today I will feed my soul at least one spiritually
nourishing morsel: prayer, a page of journaling, a
time of rest in God, worship music, a leisurely walk.

Southern Fried Chicken[1]

(real soul food)

3½ to 4 lb. chicken, cut into 8 pieces
2 cups buttermilk
1 tsp. black pepper, divided
¼ tsp. salt
1¼ cups all-purpose flour
1½ tsp. seasoned salt
1 lb. lard (or equivalent vegetable shortening)
½ cup (1 stick) butter

Step 1: Rinse the chicken pieces and blot them with paper towels. In a large bowl, combine the buttermilk, ¼ tsp. of black pepper and the salt. Stir to combine.

Step 2: Add the chicken pieces and turn to coat evenly. Cover and refrigerate for at least 2 hours or overnight, turning the pieces occasionally.

Step 3: Combine the flour, seasoned salt and the remaining ¾ tsp. of black pepper in a shallow baking dish and blend well. Line a baking sheet with three layers of paper towels and place it near the stove.

Step 4: Put the shortening and butter in a large cast-iron frying pan or pot big enough to hold the chicken pieces in one layer without touching. Melt over medium-high heat. The fat should be about ½-inch deep.

Step 5: Heat until the mixture registers 365° F on a kitchen thermometer or until a small cube of bread dropped in the oil browns in about 1 minute.

Step 6: Using tongs, remove the thighs from the marinade, draining well. Dredge them in the flour mixture, turning to coat evenly. Shake off any excess flour. Place them skin-side down in the center of the pan.

Step 7: Coat the remaining pieces in the same way and add them to the pan in a single layer without touching. Work in batches if necessary.

Step 8: Don't move the chicken for about 5 minutes or until the coating is set and looks firm. Check the underside by lifting with the tongs—it should be a deep golden color. Cook the pieces between 8 to 20 minutes (depending on size), turning them periodically until crispy brown and cooked through.

Step 9: To test, cut into the thickest part of a piece. The juices should run clear and the meat should be opaque throughout. Place on the paper-lined baking sheet to drain.

Step 10: Arrange the chicken pieces on a platter and serve hot, room temperature, or cold.

Serves 4 to 6.

Note

1. This recipe is from the Gutsy Gourmet. http://www.thegutsygourmet.net/fryed-chix.html (accessed March 28, 2006).

Section 5

FITNESS

EVEN TO YOUR OLD AGE AND GRAY HAIRS I AM HE,
I AM HE WHO WILL SUSTAIN YOU.
ISAIAH 46:4

Just mention the word "fitness" and some people have a fit! In fact, they're fit to be tied. They can't fit into their old clothing—and new clothes aren't a good fit either. But they hate pumping iron. They'd rather sit than walk or swim, and dunking donuts is certainly more fun to them than swigging a smoothie! What's a body to do?

Reform! Form new habits. Formulate a plan you can live with. Then join the line that forms to the right—right to the gym or to the track or to the

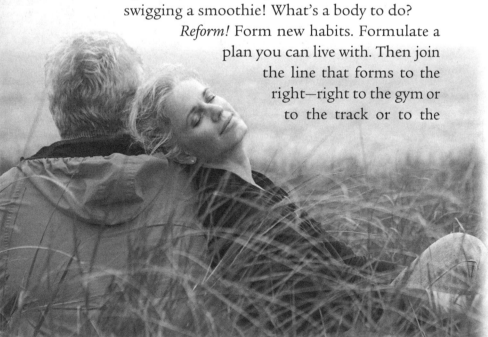

swimming pool or to the bicycle lane or to the skating arena. Give up fitful thinking and just *do* it. Think only on those things that are lovely and good and noble (see Phil. 4:8), and soon you'll be seeing those attributes in yourself— like the grandma who started running marathons at age 70 and was still running on her 90th birthday.

There are some, of course, who are *fit* with a capital *F* at any age. You know the kind: They turn your head (and even your stomach) when they walk into a room or jog through the park. Their pecs are perfect. Their biceps practically bubble. And their waists are whittled to just the right circumference. But maybe they lack a fit mind, emotional fitness or a heart fit for love.

They can change if they want to, and so can you. The opportunity to lead a life that is balanced *and* beautiful is available to anyone who wants it. So wherever you *fit*, "do what you can, with what you have, where you are." That's advice fit to live by from former U.S. president Theodore Roosevelt.

Mother (Nature)
Knows Best

My mother enjoyed reminding me of the popular phrase, "Mother knows best." She didn't always say it in words, but she made her point at various ages and stages of my life—from setting bedtimes when I was a child to establishing curfews when I was a teenager. She also introduced me to Mother Nature during my years as a Girl Scout. I will always remember our adventurous hikes through the woods, weekends at camp where I tromped through the creek in rain boots, and quiet moments sitting in the crook of a tree whittling a stick.

Those delightful experiences laid a foundation for what lay ahead. The very first time I set foot in the wilderness on a women's beginner backpack trip in the Sierra Mountains, at age 50, I knew that I had come home to Mother Nature once again.

This 50-mile one-week trek on the John Muir Trail in Yosemite National Park was my first foray into the back country of the Sierra Mountains, and I was excited about every detail. Sleeping in a tent, cooking on a small camp stove, seeing bears and ground squirrels and marmots, and hanging my laundry on tree limbs were only some of the experiences that reminded me of the pleasure of the simple life where a canteen of water, a handful of trail mix and a cozy sleeping bag were the only necessities I needed or wanted.

eyes teary with delight as we enjoy the sight of a brilliant sunset over a purple mountain?

"If we are to go forward, both as individuals and as a culture," says Chard, "we must first go back. Back to the Earth."[4] Back to Mother Nature. The truth is, we will go back eventually, "for dust you are and to dust you will return" (Gen. 3:19). But will we first return willingly to the bounty God has created and allow Him to show us, through nature, what it truly means to be a woman or man of grace, gratitude and grit—which is what being fit is all about?

GRACE
In his hand is the life of every creature and
the breath of all mankind.
(Job 12:10)

GRATITUDE
Lord, thank You for the gift of Mother Nature and all the
wonders You have created for me to learn from and to enjoy.

GRIT
This week, I will spend at least one hour with
Mother Nature—walking in a park or near a lake,
gardening, or hiking in the hills.

Notes
1. Philip Sutton Chard, *The Healing Earth* (Minocqua, WI: NorthWord Press, 1994), p. 13.
2. Ibid.
3. Ibid, p. 14.
4. Ibid.

Fit to Be Loved

Did you know that loving and being loved can boost your immune system, reduce cardiovascular disease and depression, and lead to a longer life? What an amazing prescription! Instead of looking *only* to medicines to alleviate the physical and emotional aches and pains of life, we can turn to the loving relationships we have with our mates, children, grandchildren and good friends.

Love can also inspire exercise. My husband and I joined a gym together, and we work out on the same day whenever possible. Just seeing one another across the room motivates us to keep at it. We want to be fit for our own wellbeing and also for the health of our relationship.

In her article "Ten Things Fitness Teaches You About Life," fitness expert and trainer Maria Kang suggests that as we challenge our bodies through exercise, we learn valuable lessons that apply to everyday situations with the people we love.[1]

Developing good habits with consistency and moderation, for example, and prioritizing what really matters are among the most important forms of fitness. No fitness program should ever take priority over time spent with the people we love. On the other hand, it doesn't make emotional sense to focus so much on others that we ignore our own need for exercise, rest, time alone and personal creativity.

Maria Kang also recommends that we take care of ourselves first so that we have energy left to share with others.

I like this reminder, especially as I grow older. To some it may sound selfish, but in truth it's the best gift we can give others because when we're exercised, rested, nourished and joyful, we have a basket full of blessings to share with them.

We can also break a rule every once in a while and be the better for it. For example, indulging in a bit of dark chocolate—despite its high fat and calorie content—has emotional and physical benefits to the heart, according to a recent study:

> Researchers at the University of California at Davis looked at several studies on chocolate and found that flavan-3-ols, the main flavonoids in cocoa, are associated with a decreased risk of heart disease. Dark chocolate has the highest concentration of this phytochemical, offering the best health benefits.[2]

Of course, that doesn't mean "more is better." So don't eat every piece in the box in one sitting!

Keeping our minds open to new information is also a form of fitness. As we age, it's easy to shut down and shut up. But if we remain willing to continue learning and growing in our knowledge of how to care for ourselves, then we will be vibrant, as well as interesting to be around. And we're likely to be more motivated to walk and hike and swim and play golf or to engage in whatever form of exercise appeals to us.

Fitness guru Richard Simmons adds a unique twist to the claim that love and fitness go together. He reminds his students that each of them is worthy of their own love. "You have to motivate yourself to fall in love with you," he states.[3] Unless we love and respect ourselves, all fitness and weight-loss attempts will fail.

But the most important reminder of all—the one that assures fitness for eternity—is found in the Gospel of Luke: "'Love the Lord your God with all your heart and with all your soul and with all your strength and with all your mind'; and, 'Love your neighbor as yourself'" (10:27).

GRACE
For God so loved the world that he gave his one
and only Son, that whoever believes in him
shall not perish but have eternal life.
(John 3:16)

GRATITUDE
Lord, thank You for my body, for health and fitness,
for opportunities each day to take care of myself so that I
will have plenty of vitality to share with others.

GRIT
This week, I will express self-love and love of others
by taking one action each day that contributes to
my fitness and well-being.

Notes
1. Maria Kang, "Ten Things Fitness Teaches You About Life," *Bodybuilding.com*. http://www.bodybuilding.com/fun/maria1.htm (accessed March 18, 2006).
2. "HEART SMART™: A Little Chocolate Is Good for You," *Detroit Free Press*, February 15, 2006. http://www.freep.com/apps/pbcs.dll/article?AID= /20060215/FEATURES02/602150349/1027 (accessed March 18, 2006).
3. Richard Simmons, quoted in Anne M. Russell, "How to Fall in Love with Yourself: One of Fitness's Most Enduring Veterans Offers Some Surprising Wisdom About Motivation, Weight-Loss Success and Believing in Yourself," Shape, July 2004. http://www.findarticles.com/p/ articles/mi_m0846/is_11_23/ai_n6143084 (accessed March 18, 2006).

Soul Builder

Out of curiosity, I did a Google search on the Internet to see how many links came up when I typed in the term "body builder." More than I could count! Then I did a search for the term "soul builder." I found only one— a radio show that plays uplifting Christian music. I'm tuned in now as I write this chapter.

Isn't it interesting how much emphasis our culture places on building our bodies and how little on building our souls? Yet both are important if we are to be truly fit. As I listen and write, I realize I'm building my soul. I'm filling my spirit with inspirational lyrics and music, and I can feel my heart and mind open and expand to the joy of simply praising the Lord, even as I sit here doing my day's work. There is no set format, no special set of movements, no stress or strain—and no sweat!

There are many such ways to build our souls. Listening to worship music is only one. Reading the Word is another. Praying and journaling are two more. We can also build our souls by coming clean with God when we have sin that has shut us down. At such a time, we need the cleansing breath of the Holy Spirit to blow away the dust.

King David rebuilt his soul after confessing his sins of adultery and murder. He then became one of the greatest rulers in biblical history. God gave Ruth a new

husband, Boaz, and a new life—spiritually and physically—after she was widowed and proved herself faithful to
the God of Israel. Peter had a soul-building experience
following his public denial of his relationship with Jesus.
He knew the moment the words came out of his mouth
that he had betrayed his Lord and master. But God
rebuilt him, and later he became the "rock" upon which
Jesus built His Church.

Nearly everyone experiences stops and starts when it
comes to spiritual fitness. It's part of the process of
becoming the person God made us to be. He will stand
with us. We must remain steadfast. Not give up. Not take
the easy way out—which too often ends in selling out, as
Judas did when he committed suicide or as King
Solomon did when he surrendered to pride and self-
indulgence, even after God had given him everything a
man could want: wisdom, authority and prosperity.

Staying spiritually fit, then, suggests three things to
me: first, being present to God, to myself, to others; second, settling unsettling matters quickly between God
and myself and between myself and others; and third,
speaking the truth so that I and the people around me
can be free to be our authentic selves. What does it matter how firm our body muscles are if our hearts and souls
are limp with shame or pride?

Andrew Murray, in his life-transforming book
Absolute Surrender, reminds followers of Jesus that life in
Christ is one of abiding. To build one's soul, one must
abide in Christ. "The abiding work is the work of the
heart, not of the brain, the work of the heart clinging to
and resting in Jesus, a work in which the Holy Spirit links
us to Christ Jesus."[1]

GRACE

But if from there you seek the LORD your God,
you will find him if you look for him with all
your heart and with all your soul.
(Deuteronomy 4:29)

GRATITUDE

*Lord, thank You for showing me how being a bodybuilder
and a soul builder work together for good health.*

GRIT

This week, I will do what it takes to build my body,
and I will also spend time building my soul.

Note

1. Andrew Murray, *Absolute Surrender* (Chicago, IL: Moody Press, 1980), p. 121.

Make Way for (Elder) Ducklings!

Parents of eight ducklings need a bit of help finding a safe place to raise their brood. During a rest stop in Boston's Public Garden, Mr. and Mrs. Mallard agree they just might have found the ideal spot. But soon Mrs. Mallard and her darlings become stuck on a busy street in downtown Boston. Fortunately, their policeman friend Michael rushes in, stops traffic, and makes a way for them.

And so goes the story *Make Way for Ducklings,* the children's award-winning classic by Robert McCloskey, first published by Viking Press in 1941.

Perhaps there have been times in your life when you needed someone like Policeman Michael to make a way for you. I have! Especially now that I'm older. Sometimes I feel as though I'm invisible. I want to throw up my hands and say, "Look at me. I'm a person too—an older person, I know, but still a person. Make room for me, please. Couldn't you at least acknowledge me?"

Maybe that's why I pump iron and jog and hike. I feel that if I stay buff, I won't be overlooked so easily. Maybe my age won't matter.

Well, the time came when that almost occurred. One summer morning, I jogged along the beach near my home wearing a pair of old shorts, a ratty T-shirt and a bill cap to keep my hair from flying in my face. There I was—with my naked, lined face and the rest of my body tagging along too! I didn't care what I looked like at that hour of the day.

I finished my run, wiped my face on the tail of my shirt and slowed to a walk. Just then, a teenager on a bike sailed past me and then stopped, turned around and jabbed the air with his right thumb. "Not bad for an old broad," he shouted and then pedaled out of sight.

What nerve! Who does he think I am?

Then I broke out laughing. *At least he looked. That's cool!* He was rude, but he had made a way for me that day—a way to feel good about myself just as I was.

Months later while preparing for a backpacking excursion in Yosemite, I loaded my pack with gallon-sized water bottles, pairs of tennis shoes and lots of camping gear. I was determined to get in shape for the 50-mile trek on which I'd be expected to carry a third of my weight on my back.

Up and down the hill near our home I trudged, practicing putting one foot in front of the other, day after day, panting, sweating and, yes, cussing, too.

After a week, I was feeling pretty good about myself. I was sure that I could hold my own with the other women. By the next week, I was *convinced*. Three surfer dudes cruising down the street toward the beach watched me take that hill like a pro.

"Go, Grandma, go!" Three thumbs shot up at once. I returned their approval with a thumbs-up of my own. Their encouragement made a way for me to feel good about myself and my achievement and the goal I'd set for the end of the month—to get to the top of Half Dome in Yosemite National Park.

Last year, my husband, Charles, and I were in San Simeon, California, on our way to one of my speaking engagements. One evening at dusk, we ventured out of the hotel where we were staying and walked up to the corner of Highway 1 and a cross street that led to a restaurant on the other side.

We were about to make a run for it (no traffic in either direction that we could see) when suddenly a pickup appeared. We back-stepped in surprise as it squealed to a stop. The driver leaned out the window and motioned us to cross. "Go right ahead."

Kind enough, I thought, since he was in the wrong! We stepped in front of the vehicle, waved a "thank you," and then started across.

"No problem," he called after us. "We have to take care of our older folks!"

Darn! Here I am, fit as a farmer, but to this younger generation I'm still an "older folk"!

There's something about that phrase that clangs in my ear. I'm not ready to listen to it. But maybe I should, because chronologically I am one. So I surrendered, jumped off my high horse and became willing to admit that people of any age can use a bit of support now and then. I decided to view the situation with new eyes.

That evening, the young driver had been our Policeman Michael, making a way for two elder ducklings to cross the highway safely so that we could return home the following week and get back to the gym!

GRACE

The glory of young men is their strength, gray hair
the splendor of the old. (Proverbs 20:29)

GRATITUDE

*Lord, thank You for making a way for me by Your journey
to the cross. It is the only one that really matters.*

GRIT

This week, I will take a walk or a swim, enroll in an
exercise class or join a gym. My body is a gift from
God, and I want to keep it fit for as long as I have it.

Beauty Tips

Someone once asked Audrey Hepburn to share her beauty tips. Her response was to read one of her favorite poems, written by American author and humorist Sam Levenson for his grandchild.

Time Tested Beauty Tips

For attractive lips, speak words of kindness.

For lovely eyes, seek out the good in people.

For a slim figure, share your food with the hungry.

For beautiful hair, let a child run his or her fingers through it once a day.

For poise, walk with the knowledge you'll never walk alone.

People, even more than things, have to be restored, renewed, revived, reclaimed, and redeemed; Never throw out anybody.

Remember, If you ever need a helping hand, you'll find one at the end of your arm. As you grow older, you will discover that you have two hands, one for helping yourself, the other for helping others.

The beauty of a woman is not in the clothes she wears, the figure that she carries, or the way she combs her hair. The beauty of a woman must be seen from in her eyes, because that is the doorway to her heart, the place where love resides.

The beauty of a woman is not in a facial mole, but true beauty in a woman is reflected in her soul. It is the caring that she lovingly gives, the passion that she shows, and the beauty of a woman with passing years only grows![1]

I love this poem. It not only speaks of physical fitness but of emotional and spiritual fitness as well. It's an excellent reminder that even though we want to remain attractive and vibrant in our later years, such a look does not come from workouts and diet alone. Our behavior and attitude are essential to the whole package.

I was inspired by a few older folks I "met" while reading an article by Sarah Mahoney in *AARP Magazine*. Every person the author interviewed was 85 years of age or older, and all agreed that stress makes you old.

For Pauline "Dully" Kirn, age 90, playing bridge is what keeps her mentally fit. She and others find that playing mind-challenging games benefits them almost as much as those who focused on physical exercise alone.

Ernest Brown, known as "Brownie," age 88, has been tap-dancing since the '30s and '40s. He's currently part of a two-man tap-dancing act that performs around the country. For him, humor is the key. It zaps stress. Those who can meet life with laughter are likely to live longer and more happily, and Brownie is living proof.

For Bob Brown, age 95, having a sense of purpose makes the difference between feeling fit and feeling useless. Work is the answer for him—though it must be an endeavor he's passionate about. "Right now, it's watercolors," he says. In previous years, he was a master leather carver and was distinguished for crafting holsters for Hopalong Cassidy, Montgomery Clift and John Wayne. Brown also attributes his long life to clean living. "I don't smoke, I don't drink, I don't carouse," he says.

Grace Nunery, age 86, says, "I don't worry about anything, and I pray about everything." Today, she continues a ministry to the deaf that she started 50 years ago. Since that time, her ministry has expanded to a summer camp program for deaf children, drawing attendees from around the world. Grace quotes her favorite verse from the Bible: "Don't worry about anything, pray about everything, and always be thankful" (see 1 Thess. 5:16-18).[2]

Imagine how fit we'd all feel if we gave up worry, prayed about all things and focused on being grateful!

GRACE
Enter his gates with thanksgiving and his courts
with praise; give thanks to him and praise his name.
(Psalm 100:4)

GRATITUDE
*Lord, thank You for the guidance of Your Word and the
joy that comes from walking with You.*

GRIT
This week, I will list those activities that bring me
happiness and contentment, and I'll spend at least
30 minutes a day enjoying one of them.

Notes
1. Sam Levenson, "Time Tested Beauty Tips," *In One Era and Out the Other* (New York: Simon and Schuster, 1973), n.p.
2. Sarah Mahoney, "10 Secrets of a Good, Long Life," *AARP Magazine* (July/August 2005), pp. 47-54.

Time Out

I went out of town for the weekend, eager for a getaway, time with friends, and a visit with my son. As I sailed north on the freeway from my home, I remembered a sign that I had seen in the past: Rest Area Ahead. I watched for the sign intently. I needed a bathroom break and a stretch. My right thigh was cramping, and I was feeling a little bleary-eyed—a sure indicator that it was time to pull over and get refreshed.

Suddenly there was the sign—just in the nick of time. I worked my way over to the exit ramp, and then cruised into the Rest Area and followed the arrow pointing to the aisle for autos. I slid out, took care of urgent business, and then power-walked for 10 minutes. A swig of cold water, a handful of nuts to munch and a 10-minute nap in the car and I was as good as new, ready for the next hundred miles.

As I sat behind the driver's wheel, I saw how much this simple time-out had refreshed my mind and spirit. I then decided to make this a regular stop on all my trips north and south. It's the smart thing to do, I realized. What is the point of rushing, of pushing, of stressing?

When I think of the word "fitness" or see it in print, I usually associate it with some form of exercise—the more cardiac-oriented the better. But is that the only description of the word? I mulled that over a bit and came to a new perspective: A fit body—or a fit life, for that matter—should also include times and places in which we come to a full stop, even if only for a few minutes.

That doesn't mean we should give up the activities we love—trips to the gym, walks in the park, volleyball on the beach, square dancing, a round of golf. All these and more contribute to overall fitness. But we also might consider the importance of time-outs—not the kind for misbehavior, but the kind that ensures good behavior and good health.

Then we can lift ourselves up by our bootstraps, jump to conclusions, pull our own load, climb the walls, bend over backwards, jump on the bandwagon, run in circles, and start the ball rolling! After all that, it'll be time to hang loose and rest and recuperate all over again.

GRACE
You will be secure, because there is hope; you will
look about you and take your rest in safety.
(Job 11:18)

GRATITUDE
Lord, I thank You for reminding me that a time-out
is as important to my well-being as exercise.

GRIT
Today, when I feel fatigued, I'll stop what I'm doing
and take a time-out without guilt or apology.

Section 6

FINANCES

*BUT REMEMBER THE Lord YOUR GOD, FOR IT IS HE WHO
GIVES YOU THE ABILITY TO PRODUCE WEALTH.*
DEUTERONOMY 8:18

Money, money! Cunning, conniving, confusing! Like food, we can't live without it, but it sure can be hard to live with. Advertisers lure us with every conceivable message and image: "You deserve it." "Buy now, pay later." "You *can* have it all." And they cast the line even further to catch the retiree, the senior, the elderly.

How about this one: "Your house wants to give you a vacation" the ad reads, followed by an invitation to take cash from a home equity line to

sail off to the Bahamas! Of course, there is no mention of the fact that you'll be borrowing from yourself, taking from your future and setting yourself up for another payment plan when perhaps your home has been paid off for years.

"Prosperity," according to financial coach Jerry Gellis, "is living easily and happily in the real world, whether you have money or not." Getting a grip on your finances while keeping a grip on yourself is not easy, but you can do it. It takes strength of character, a sound mind and a willingness to stay rooted in Christ's teachings. "Better one hand with tranquility than two handfuls with toil and chasing after the wind" (Eccles. 4:6).

See the writings in this section for more on the merry-go-round of money. If you have your finances under control, there is plenty here to encourage you to keep at it.

Money Mania

Mary Ellen controls her adult children and grandchildren through spending. Anton spends in order to change his lonely feelings since his wife died. Roz plays dumb regarding her finances because she fears the power of money. Garth gambles; he bets on the horses and buys a lottery ticket every week.

The merry-go-round of financial debt, dependence and despair whirls these men and women 'round and around. How and why they continue the ride is a complex issue. For some older people, the attention they receive from others when they buy items is the key. Buying products from the shopping channel gives them a chance to speak with the presenter or the creator over the phone. They like the compliments and the encouragement they receive.

For others, purchasing expensive gifts for friends and family gives them a rush. They are providing what perhaps no one else can. Still others like being vague about the state of their affairs. "What I don't know, I don't worry about," said one woman. "Denial is a beautiful thing," joked a man in heavy debt. All of these people behave in ways that diminish and demean themselves, and they don't know how to stop it.

My own money-mania ride began the year I married my first husband. We were living in a furnished one-bedroom apartment and had everything we needed except a television set. We bought one on credit. It was so easy—so simple in fact that for the next 20 years, we were never again out of debt. We were addicted to instant gratification, to living beyond our means. It took me another 10 years following our divorce to admit my part in the problem and to change my behavior.

What happens? How do we get this way? And why? I doubt that any of us chooses—at least consciously—to be irresponsible with money. It's not a decision we make, like taking art lessons or planning a vacation or joining a church. That's why it's so insidious. All we know is that we are miserable around money and that we want to change.

The challenge in wanting to change our behavior, however, is being impatient and naïve about the process. We didn't get this way overnight, and we won't get out of it overnight. But we can pay attention to how we use (and abuse) money so that we can gain some understanding of how this problem occurs. It usually starts with the little things:

- Buying items we don't need or even want
- Shopping to make ourselves feel better
- Jeopardizing our financial health to help others
- Gambling to relieve stress

If you feel uncomfortable with money and know that you're using it to feel better or different about yourself, it may help to think about it in a new way. Ultimately, money is simply another of the many blessings God has provided. He alone is the source of our supply and the owner of all that we have. He has always taken care of us and always will. "What I have said, that will I bring about; what I have planned, that will I do" (Isa. 46:11).

As soon as the truth of those words penetrates your heart, you can begin to take your financial habits in hand and then step off the merry-go-round. Getting started includes looking at the following four truths that ultimately lead to success:

1. *Face the truth about yourself.* Admitting your behavior first to yourself and then to God is crucial. Then it's time to roll up your shirt sleeves and dig in. For example, if you suffer from a gambling addiction, you will need to join a support group such as Debtors Anonymous or Gamblers Anonymous, where you will receive love and accountability.

2. *Discover the truth about God.* As I embarked on my search for the truth about myself, I became aware of the void at the center of my life—a hole that had been there for many years, but one which I was just beginning to notice and feel. I was to discover in the months ahead that this missing element was the truth about God. Before that moment, I had never fully embraced the fact that He died for me so that my sins could be forgiven, so that I could have the abundant life He promised in John 10:10: "My purpose is to give life in all its fullness" (*TLB*).

3. *Learn the truth about others.* Everyone has a deep hunger for the fellowship and forgiveness of God. We can help each other overcome our difficulties by recognizing that we are not alone. As you support another person, you also support yourself.

4. *Apply the truth to your life.* Life has pain and problems. We'll never be totally free of them. But the Lord promises to remain with us through all of our trials. In 1 Peter 5:7, we are reminded to "let him have all your worries and cares, for he is always thinking about you and watching everything that concerns you" (*TLB*). How reassuring!

It is my deep conviction, from my own life and from speaking with others, that there can be no lasting change unless and until we are willing to take action on our behalf and receive support—through prayer, the counsel of someone we trust, and a regular, safe place to share our worries, fears and feelings as we step off the merry-go-round.

Real change is about entrusting our lives and our situations to God. It's about getting ourselves right spiritually and emotionally so that we can use practical tools in a God-directed way. It's about laying up treasure in heaven, not on Earth, "for where your treasure is, there will your heart be also" (Matt. 6:21).

GRACE
Whoever trusts in his riches will fall, but the
righteous will thrive like a green leaf.
(Proverbs 11:28)

GRATITUDE
Dear God, I thank You that You always provide.

GRIT
Today, I choose to look at my habits around money
and to find a person or a group that will support
healthy behavior and help me become accountable.

The Bible Tells Us So

The Christmas tree is down, the decorations have been put away, the gifts have been accepted or exchanged, the thank-you notes are written, and the last piece of fruitcake is finally gone! It's time to start fresh. It's a brand-new year. For many, however and maybe you're among them January is a bummer because the credit card bills arrive. Now it's time to pay for all the holiday spending, especially for all the items we purchased for our children and grandchildren. Will you make a minimum payment and let the debt slide till next month, or will you gather the courage to pay it all off and then cut up the cards and live on a cash basis? A tough decision either way.

Owe No Man (or Woman)

The Bible tells us to owe no man (or woman), for "the borrower is servant to the lender" (Prov. 22:7). And yet we do! One couple I know paid $200,000 in cash for a small beach apartment. They were so happy to own their home free and clear. Within a year, however, they had opened a home equity line of credit, and 12 months later, after purchasing a car and going on two cruises, they were $100,000 in debt!

Susan Walker, finance writer and investor relations executive, states in an article for Foxnews.com that the use of credit has taken off dramatically in the United States since 1990. "While the number of people holding charge cards grew about 75 percent—from 82 million in 1990 to 144 million in 2003—the amount they charged during that period grew by a much larger percentage: approximately 350 percent, from $338 billion to $1.5 trillion."[1]

The ease of buying on credit, refinancing a piece of property and using credit cards instead of cash for even basic necessities encourages us to put off till tomorrow what should be paid for today. In doing so, it's easy to lose all sense of what is right, just, healthy and sensible. So what are we to do?

Look to the Bible

For the past 10 years, Kathy Miller, prosperity coach and founder of agoodsteward.net, has been helping men and women of all ages put their financial houses in order. She not only teaches her clients how to eliminate debt and regain control over their finances, but she also reminds them of the guidance and grace on this topic that is available in the Bible. Only with God's help can any of us have lasting success.

Miller encourages men and women to consider the following verses in conjunction with these practical steps as they face their debt, seek help and rely on the Lord to keep them focused and committed to financial health and peace of mind:

1. *Put all details regarding your money in front of you in a consistent easy-to-read format.* "What is impossible with men is possible with God" (Luke 18:27). God knows the truth about your finances, so even if you feel overwhelmed or frightened about facing the truth, commit to seeing it through.

The Lord will not fail you. Bring out your check-book, your bills, your investment statements, your paycheck stubs and so on. Then put every-thing in writing. Kathy Miller's workbook *A Good Steward's Journal: The Busy Christian's Guide to Better Money Management* (available from www.agood steward.net) is an excellent tool for this purpose.

2. *Organize your time and space.* "Each one should use whatever gift he has received to serve others, faith-fully administering God's grace in its various forms" (1 Pet. 4:10). We are more likely to make impulsive purchases when we are out of time, feel-ing disorganized or frantic with worry. We pick up an outfit we think we need because we don't know what's in our closet. We spend more on gifts and restaurants and frivolous entertainment than is prudent for the income we have. We give in to our feelings instead of planning ahead.

However, the moment we bring order and peace to our time and surroundings, creativity and energy will become available, and we'll be able to accomplish things we only dreamed of before. At such times, the talents and gifts of others can be a Godsend. Consider hiring a pro-fessional organizer to help you get started. Visit www.organizingpro.com for some great ideas and a free weekly e-zine from Marcia Ramsland, president of Life Management Skills.

3. *Eliminate mental and emotional clutter.* "Now faith is being sure of what we hope for and certain of what we don't see" (Heb. 11:1). Cloudy thinking,

past beliefs and addictive behaviors such as overeating, gambling or excessive shopping can keep us locked in financial and emotional debt. We often use money to avoid painful feelings, as well as the truth about ourselves and the truth about God.

Sometimes a few sessions with a professional coach, counselor and/or an accountability partner or support group can help you get started on this internal housecleaning that will lead to a new and healthy relationship with money. These groups may include Debtors Anonymous, Overcomers Outreach, Al-Anon family groups, or Codependents Anonymous (CODA)—all of which are modeled after the original support program of Alcoholics Anonymous. Contact information for these organizations is available in a city telephone directory or on the Internet.

4. *Bring peace and balance to your life.* "Let no debt remain outstanding, except the continuing debt to love one another, for he who loves his fellow-man has fulfilled the law" (Rom. 13:8). Make time (don't wait for it to appear) for prayer and meditation, regular exercise, deep breathing, reflection, reading and tithing (giving at least 10 percent of your earnings, no matter how small, to a charity or church of your choice).

"When you're in survival, you can't share your gifts," says Miller. "It's essential to give to others even as you are giving to yourself (and working your way out of debt). Tithing works for everyone. As you give you receive."[2] And as you give, you are less likely to fall into the debt trap because you will have a new and beautiful way of viewing and using money—as a means of exchange and provision, not as a way to indulge yourself or escape reality.

Money and possessions ultimately are not ours anyway but gifts from God. Perhaps that recognition and acceptance are the most important lessons of all.

GRACE
Of what use is money in the hand of a fool,
since he has no desire to get wisdom?
(Proverbs 17:16)

GRATITUDE
*Dear God, I thank You for showing me the
light regarding my finances.*

GRIT
Today, I will face the bills that need to be paid—
and establish a plan for paying them.

Notes
1. Susan Walker, "U.S. Consumer Credit Card Debt May Crash Economy," *FoxNews.com*, December 31, 2004. http://www.foxnews.com/story/0,2933,143037,00.html (accessed March 18, 2006).
2. Kathy Miller, *A Good Steward's Journal: The Busy Christian's Guide to Better Money Management* (Stirling, NJ: A Good Steward, 2004), n.p.

In Search of Rest

Our society creates an insatiable hunger for action and acquisition. If we're not out there shopping till we drop, dining till we're stuffed or spending till we're broke, we may feel un-American!

It takes raw courage to turn away from the lure of our consumer-oriented culture, which is consumed with consuming! But when we do, we often get to the bottom of our true desires: a chance to kick back, relax and do nothing except sit at the feet of Jesus and enjoy His companionship. That sounds delicious to me. And it's *free*. No cost. No interest. No payment plan. Consider what awaits you when you invest your time, instead of your money, in what really matters—being still and knowing God.

Rest from Burdens

"Come to me, all you who are weary and burdened, and I will give you rest" (Matt. 11:28). Merchants don't want you to rest. They want you to buy their goods and services. Bankers don't want you to rest. They want to loan you money so that they can charge you interest. Friends don't want you to rest. They want you to go to a ballgame or a party.

Only the Lord wants you to rest. Only He wants you to come away with Him when you are weary and burdened. When you hear His call, put down whatever you're doing. Follow His lead, whether it's to the hammock for a nap or to the park for a leisurely walk.

Rest from People

"Then, because so many people were coming and going that they did not even have a chance to eat, He said to them, 'Come with me by yourselves to a quiet place and get some rest'" (Mark 6:31).

My husband walked through the front door one December evening, tossed his jacket and keys on the chair in the hallway and let out a big sigh. "I've had enough of people," he said, obviously wiped out after a long day behind the customer-service counter at the store where he worked at the time. "This is supposed to be a happy time of year. But people are impatient, angry, in a hurry. I'll be glad when it's all over."

Some relaxing music, a few moments of prayer together and a good night's sleep helped Charles get back to normal. Like Jesus, he felt the press of the crowd and needed to retreat for a few hours. How much our lives would change for the better if we, like Jesus, did what our heavenly Father tells us to do: rest from people.

Rest in the Lord

"He who dwells in the shelter of the Most High will rest in the shadow of the Almighty" (Ps. 91:1). What an awesome truth to contemplate. Those who trust in the Lord will experience His protection—over their finances, families, responsibilities at work, and their very lives. If we seek God first, build our lives in and through Him and put Him above everything else, He will provide for our every need and the needs of those in our care.

How could we turn down such an invitation? God is our dwelling place and our plane of refuge and rest. Retreat to Him often during the autumn and winter of your life, and allow Him to refresh your spirit, renew your mind and refuel your body. You deserve it!

GRACE

My soul finds rest in God alone; my
salvation comes from him.
(Psalm 62:1)

GRATITUDE

Dear God, I thank You for calling me to a time of rest.

GRIT

Today, I will spend at least one hour in rest,
regardless of the items on my to-do list!

31 Simple Treats

Here's a list of simple treats to hang on your wall, pin to a corkboard or tape to your bathroom mirror. There are enough of them for an entire month. And notice that most of them don't require any money. These are wonderful ways to experience your personal wealth—the kind that has little to do with finances. Enjoy!

1. Invite a new neighbor in for afternoon tea and conversation.
2. Meet a new or old friend or business colleague for a lunchtime walk—exercise and conversation without calories.
3. Give your spouse a foot rub or a back massage before bed to help him or her unwind. The next night, it's your turn!
4. Walk barefoot on the grass in the early morning—an invigorating wakeup call to your body, although I don't recommend doing this in winter if you live in snow country!
5. Visit a library and browse the shelves. Pick a book that is just right for this moment in your life. Take it home and read it. Then recommend it to a friend.
6. Choose a recipe you haven't made for a while. Roll up your sleeves and produce it to enjoy with your spouse, grandchild, adult child or a friend.
7. Call someone you haven't seen in several weeks

or months. Chat and reconnect.

8. Send a note, a postcard or greeting card to six people in your address book—just to say hello and to
let them know that you are thinking of them today.

9. Take a leisurely salt bath, and then take a nap.

10. Place a photo of someone you love on your dress-
er. Look at it each day and pray for that person.

11. Jot down in your day planner or in a notebook all
of the blessings you received today. Revisit the
list a week from now and see how rich you are.

12. Purchase a medley of fresh fruits and make a big
fruit salad. Then feast on this healthy food and
notice how good you feel afterward.

13. Call your children or your nieces and nephews
on the phone and tell them you love them.

14. Stand in front of the mirror and declare out
loud two positive things that you notice about
yourself.

15. Take a risk. Tell someone the truth you've been
withholding; compliment someone you admire.

16. Volunteer at the local hospital, Girl Scouts or Boy
Scouts, church youth group or local government.

17. Be creative. Bake a fancy cake. Arrange dried
flowers in a pretty basket. Sew. Knit. Make jewelry. Draw. Sketch. Carve something from wood.

18. Start a joy journal. Write down today and each day
this month one thing you have to be happy about.

19. Plan your summer vacation. Take one step
toward making it happen.

20. Purchase a new blouse or shirt in a bold pattern
or color that makes you smile.

21. Toss or give away all clothing you haven't worn
in the past two years.

22. Start a gift-giving fund. Put away a dollar or two a day and you'll have a bit of cash when you need it for a birthday or holiday present.
23. Veg for a day! (It's okay to take time out to sit and stare.)
24. Drink eight glasses of water today. Notice how you feel when you're fully hydrated.
25. Smile at everyone you meet today. Pay attention to who smiled back!
26. Allow someone else to have the last word—even when you deserve it.
27. Listen to classical music while driving.
28. Ask for help when you need it. It's a joy to share a burden.
29. Balance your bank account. Oh, the relief you'll feel!
30. Comfort someone in need.
31. Say or write an original prayer of thanks each day for a month—and then do it for another month.

GRACE

You have made known to me the path of life;
you will fill me with joy in your presence, with
eternal pleasures at your right hand.
(Psalm 16:11)

GRATITUDE

*Dear God, I thank You for encouraging me to have
fun without spending money I don't have.*

GRIT

Today, I will begin a month of treats, choosing one
each day from the list above and ending each day
with a prayer of thanks.

Stay-at-Home Vacations

How would you like to save money on hotels, restaurants and airfare and still enjoy a first-class vacation—alone, with your spouse or your family? "Who wouldn't?" you might ask.

My husband and I did just that one summer following the purchase of a new home. We had little money for extras at that point, but plenty of desire to have fun, especially after the stress of moving an entire household.

We came up with a plan that involved everyone. First, we blocked out five days in July and then planned a different outing for each day in and around the city of Los Angeles, where we lived at the time. Everyone in the family had a say in what we did. For example, my son wanted to go to the beach. My oldest daughter wanted to visit the historical ship the *Queen Mary*. My youngest child wanted to go to Disneyland. We also made time for a museum—my choice— and for a sporting event for my husband.

With our plan in hand, we then talked about food. To save money and time, we decided to eat breakfast at home, pack a picnic lunch to enjoy at a park, and eat dinner at a restaurant. By the end of the week, we all agreed that it had been one of the most memorable vacations we'd ever had—stress-free, fiscally responsible, and fun! The best part was being together in a way that worked for everyone.

This can work for two people, an entire family or for grandparents and grandkids—wherever you are in life. "I really like doing things as a family," said my son. And that statement came from an adolescent who had appeared to be breaking away from family traditions!

If you'd like to plan a simple, stay-at-home vacation for you and your family, here are some ways to make it happen:

- Block out a period of time—from a weekend to a full week.

- Establish a vacation budget.

- Gather your family around and make a list of places you'd like to see and experiences you'd like to have. When you finish, you'll know which ones drew the best reactions. Some of your family members may like one or two items on the list and not the others. For example, preschoolers are not likely to think looking at artwork is fun. On the other hand, a teen will not be thrilled to go to a toddler's park. To avoid conflict, assure each person that at least one of their choices will be honored. This can make all the difference between family harmony and disharmony. It can also be an opportunity to learn to give and take.

- Delegate various tasks, such as gathering brochures, loading the camera, mapping out the driving route or planning the picnic lunch. Depending on the age of your children or grandchildren, there is likely to be at least one action each person can take to contribute to the vacation.

At the end of the week, share your most memorable moments and look at your photos. I'd be willing to bet that everyone will already be anticipating next year's simple, stay-at-home vacation.

GRACE

Go, eat your food with gladness, and drink
your wine with a joyful heart, for it is now
that God favors what you do.
(Ecclesiastes 9:7)

GRATITUDE

*Dear God, I thank You for the opportunity to have
time with my family in joyful pursuits.*

GRIT

Today, I will think about a vacation that will be fun for
my whole family without breaking the bank!

More Moola

My husband has developed a habit of stopping a few mornings each week at a local bagelry for coffee and a copy of *USA Today*. Sometimes he also picks up an onion bagel with cream cheese, and sometimes he's content with a cup of java by itself. True, he could have his coffee at home for a lot less money, but there's something about the buzz and busyness of this corner shop that helps him start his day on a happy note.

And that's where money meets the mind. When is it appropriate to eat or drink at home, thereby saving a few bucks, and when is it just fine to spend that pocket change on a treat? I have no idea. It seems to be a matter of taste and temperament. Some people love to save and others love to spend—whether a couple of dollars for a coffee and croissant or for a slice of pizza and a bottle of pop.

We all, however, can do a few small things to hang on to more of our hard-earned moola while still giving in *once in a while* to our small passions, such as a movie, a new CD, a pair of earrings, the latest handyman tool or a hard-back novel.

Here are some ideas to consider and apply if they appeal to you.

Pay Bills Online

With the cost of postage rising, it is becoming even more imperative to look for ways to avoid spending so much on stamps. If your household receives 10 bills a month and you pay each one by snail mail, your cost of postage is $3.90 per month, or $46.80 per year. If you switch to online bill paying (where there is no cost to you), you are then free to put the money you save on postage into a gift account, give it to charity, or add it to your savings account.

Eat at Home More Often

Even if you catch an early-bird special or a senior-discount dinner, you'll still spend $50 to $75 for two meals. The dinner may be a modest charge, but add an appetizer, wine with dinner and coffee and dessert, and you're up there. You might decide, instead, to eat out just one or two nights a month or save such an expenditure for special occasions such as a birthday, Valentine's Day or your wedding anniversary.

Another good compromise my husband and I have found is sharing a meal. (Of course, if you can't agree on what to order, that shortcut to savings won't work.) In general, the portions restaurants serve are larger than anyone needs to eat. When two people share a meal, there is no waste, and the bill is within reason. Another option is to go out for lunch instead of dinner. Prices and portions are often smaller for noontime meals. Less food and fewer calories are better for your waistline—and your wallet, as well.

Soap Up and Rinse Off

One of the largest undetected household expenses is water. Turn off the tap while you wash your face, brush your teeth or get undressed for a shower or bath. In the kitchen, rinse dishes in a small plastic tub, and then stack in the dishwasher instead of turning the faucet on and off for each item or letting water run while rinsing.

To conserve water outdoors, water plants in the early morning so that the moisture goes to the roots quickly instead of evaporating. These and other sound tips, according to the National Rural Water Association, can save you $189 a year off the average U.S. household's annual water bill of $476. (For more water-saving tips, take the Home Tour at www.h2ouse.org.)

Track Your Expenditures

For nearly 20 years, I have been writing in a small notebook, which I carry in my purse, the money I spend with cash, check or debit card. At the end of each week, I transfer those numbers to the appropriate category in my expenditures file on my computer—e.g., groceries, fuel, medical appointments, restaurant meals, car wash, clothing, and so on.

This one seemingly insignificant task has changed my relationship with money. I am now completely aware of what I earn, spend, save and give away. And because I know that I am going to write down the expenses, I am more thoughtful about what I purchase. I am less impulsive and more conservative. I plan my spending and carry with me only the amount of money I need. This simple practice has given me insight into my emotions and moods and how I've used money in the past (and sometimes now) to cope with discomfort or fear.

I have also become an expert at delayed gratification. I don't give in to my urges as quickly as I used to. I pause, think about what I want to buy—whether a fruit smoothie on a hot day or a new dress for a special party—and *choose* to make the purchase when it's prudent and satisfying. I've found that I now return home with more moola in my wallet and more peace in my mind and heart.

GRACE

The man who had received the five talents
went at once and put his money to
work and gained five more.
(Matthew 25:16)

GRATITUDE

*God, I thank You for not only providing for my needs,
but also for being my very provision.*

GRIT

Today, I will look for a way to use my money wisely
so that I will have enough to take care of my needs
and some to save for another time.

FUN

*SHOUTS OF JOY AND VICTORY RESOUND IN THE
TENTS OF THE RIGHTEOUS.*
PSALM 118:15

My husband is the same age as Mickey Mouse. Charles was born in October 1928 in Paducah, Kentucky, of Ada and Charlie Flowers. Mickey was born early in 1928 in the imagination of Walt Disney during a train ride from New York to Los Angeles with his wife. So when my husband and I think of doing something fun together, going to Disneyland is among the top 10 on our list. As I write this, we are planning a trip there for Charles's birthday this year.

This is just one example of ways to bring out the child in yourself and another, so important at any time in life but even more so as we grow older. Don't let go of the kid inside! Bring him or her out to play every day and several times a year. Extend the time to a couple of days or a week or, if you have the option, even a month. Playtime does not have to be expensive or, for that matter, cost anything at all. Mr. or Ms. Anonymous once said, "We don't stop having fun when we're old; we're old when we stop having fun."

So don't put off playing till tomorrow when today is all you can be sure of. Find out more about playing in the writings in this section.

Get It on Paper!

"Isn't this fun, Gramma? Just the two of us?" My eight year-old grandson, Noah, hopped out of the car and onto a nearby rock and then onto a log and then onto a picnic table and then onto another rock. The fun had begun. We had just arrived at a Nature Knowledge Workshop for kids, parents and grandparents in the Laguna Mountains in Southern California.

I had signed up because I thought it would be a week-end of fun for Noah. And it was. But to my surprise it was a lot of fun for me too! I loved the nature walks, the hikes, the rock climbing, the delicious food and the cozy rustic room where we slept in sleeping bags on bunk beds.

One of the most significant activities of the weekend for Noah was journal writing. I would not have expected that keeping a journal would be fun for an eight-year-old, but I was wrong. He got into it.

He asked me to help him make a few entries in a science journal that he had started at home with his mother, who is also his homeschool teacher. He wanted some tangible memories of our weekend together learning about animals and plants.

Noah unpacked his journal first thing and made sure he had it with him at all times. As soon as we completed a hike or a walk or a lecture, he pulled it out, handed it to me and then dictated three or four sentences that summarized his experience. I wrote down exactly what he said. He's an excellent reader, but at the time he was still mastering his writing skills.

Noah could then add personal drawings or photos or pictures from magazines to illustrate his entries. After viewing a slide show on animal behavior, he asked me to write the following: "If you see a mountain lion, don't run. Make yourself look big by putting your arms over your head and pushing out your muscles."

By Sunday afternoon, he had several pages filled with writing and simple drawings. When we met his dad at our usual rendezvous spot, the first words out of Noah's mouth were "Dad, Dad, want to hear my journal?"

His father later reported that Noah read from his science journal all the way home. And he entertained and informed his brothers and sister at dinner with all the new facts he had learned at the Nature Knowledge Workshop.

I had captured most of our experiences on film, so I sent him a small photo album of pictures to augment his science journal. It was a rich experience for both of us. We shared a very special time together as grandmother and grandson, and we also learned more about God's green earth and the bounty of natural gifts He's provided. And because of Noah's journal, he has it not only in his heart and mind but on paper as well.

You might consider doing something similar with your grandchildren. Help them capture their experiences and interests in words. Then have fun together adding colorful stickers, smiley faces and personal artwork such as drawings, sketches and photos with captions. Your grandchildren can make this a personal journal or they can begin one for the family or for a friend, jotting down experiences they've shared, adventures they've enjoyed with you and others, or writing notes about whatever they're interested in.

An important part of growing older with grace, gratitude and grit is making time for fun with the young people in our lives—whether grandchildren, nieces and nephews or neighbor kids. We have much to offer them and they have much to offer us. We may not be able to climb a mountain or play touch football with them, but we can encourage their creativity and their sensitivity as they enjoy life, capture it in words and then get it on paper!

GRACE
Write down the revelation and make it plain on
tablets so that a herald may run with it.
(Habakkuk 2:2)

GRATITUDE
*Lord, I thank You for the gift of words. I always
feel better when I express in writing what is in my
heart and on my mind. I look forward to sharing
this gift with my grandchildren.*

GRIT
Today, I will spend at least 10 minutes free-writing
whatever is on my mind—and enjoy the experience.

Funny Side Up

Remember the old song "The Sunny Side of the Street"? The lyricist invites listeners to grab their coats and hats, put their worries on their doorstep, and then step right up to the sunny side of the street—where life can be so sweet.

Of course, if you're having a down day, such words can be downright annoying! Life feels like anything but sweet or good at such a time. Yet even then, you have the power to turn your attitude toward gratitude. And as you give thanks for life itself, you might be surprised at how you brighten up and see not only the sunny side again but even the funny side.

It happened to me this week. I had three or four days in a row when I felt grumpy, ungrateful and fearful. My husband and I are facing a major change in our life, and I realized that I don't have any control over the order in which the details play out. I've done my part. The rest is up to God. You'd think I'd be happy to turn all my worries over to Him, but I'm not. I'm ambivalent. I'm scared. I'm a little nuts right now. I want to know what's going on behind the scenes and how He'll work it all out. Nosy me!

When I got fed up being anxious, I decided to take my own advice and be grateful instead. I thanked God for taking care of me and my petty problems and for guiding me to make fruitful decisions that will be in our best interest. The more I expressed my gratitude, the lighter and better I felt. Soon I was smiling. My heart was calm. I even laughed out loud at my previous foolishness. I was once again walking down the sunny, funny side of the street—regardless of the uncertainty ahead. Because I can't change what I'm not in charge of, I decided to come back to the moment, view things from a positive point of view and live my life funny side up!

Getting creative can help. When we express ourselves through music, art, writing, dance or crafts, we lighten up and loosen up. We laugh more easily and we feel more playful. In other words, being creative is fun.

Maybe as you read this you're feeling a familiar longing overcome you. You ache to be heard and let out the music or lyrics that burn inside, the painting you can already envision, the scenes you've photographed in your heart a million times or the poem or story you've completed in your mind. Don't ignore that feeling. Decide now to take that first step on the sunny side of the street and see where it leads.

Start small. Take one step toward your goal. Instead of focusing on the grandiose (writing a best-selling novel, becoming a world-famous concert violinist), "take the small but necessary first steps," says my friend and creativity coach, Earl Storm. When you think only of results, you miss the best part. If you want to write, enroll in a class on writing for publication or buy a blank book and begin a journal. If you've always wanted to play the piano, rent one, and then invest in some lessons and see how you feel after that.

Allow small mistakes. Expect to make mistakes and then learn from them. "For years, my life was an intense roller-coaster ride," says Earl. "I was either elated or depressed. I wanted to find a middle ground where I could live comfortably and do my art." Earl said he realized that it was okay to make a mistake, to create a drawing and toss it out, to send out a cartoon strip and get it back. Most creative people admit that mistakes are part of the process of personal expression. They don't let rejection spoil their fun.

Take small breaks. Stop and reflect. Rest and breathe. "From time to time, step away from the doing of your art," Earl suggests, "and notice the creativity around you—other people's art, and the art in nature. We need to fill our well. Time-outs are as important to the process as the art itself." Doing nothing for a short period may be just what is called for to restore your enthusiasm and fun.

Celebrate small triumphs. Keep a scrapbook of your progress. "Victories are much more than parades and confetti," says Earl. "Those that really count are quiet and deeply personal." Just finishing a poem or a song or a painting or a quilt is a victory worth noting. Maybe that piece of art has been going round and round in your mind and heart for years. Now it's on paper or canvas or on the wall. You are no longer thinking about it. It's there in front of you to look at and feel and read and admire. Cause for celebration. It's time for a date with the artist within you! Plan something fun, something you'll really enjoy.

Recognize how small steps lead to larger life. Are you ready to embark on your own creative venture? Are you ready to have fun unleashing your talent? Consider these steps:

- Activate your imagination. *Dream.* What have you always wanted to do? Paint? Write? Sing? Dance? Design?

- Find a safe place to air any fears you have: a good friend, a journal, a support group of like-minded people.

• Take the necessary next step. Buy a book about your art, enroll in a class, hire a coach or mentor, talk with people who have gone before you.

• Give yourself permission and time and space simply to create. Keep looking at the sunny side of the street, where there's light and laughter and lots of loving support.

GRACE

For the LORD your God will bless you in all your harvest and in all the work of your hands, and your joy will be complete.
(Deuteronomy 16:15)

GRATITUDE

Lord, I am grateful today for the work of Your hands in my life, for giving me talent and opportunity. May I always use my gifts for good.

GRIT

Today, I will leave my worries on my doorstep and spend the day on the sunny, funny side of the street.

You Can Do That!

Easy for you, I told my inner self as I stood in front of a group of 300 women at a retreat at which I was the weekend speaker. I had been talking about the importance of letting go, having fun, giving in to the playful side, fulfilling a long-held goal, taking a risk. I realized that I had done all of those things in my life, so it was no big deal for me to speak about them openly to others. But maybe it wasn't so easy for some of them to take a brave step in their lives. So I decided to offer an opportunity for volunteers to declare the one thing they'd always wanted to do but had not yet done.

I was thrilled with the response I received. One young woman stood up and said that she longed to sing in front of people. She had held back because of fear and shyness. That day, she declared in front of 300 women that she would start vocal lessons and join a community choral group. The room erupted in applause, and then she and her mother, who was sitting next to her, burst into happy tears and hugs. The singer within had been set free.

Next, a mother of three adult children raised her hand. "I'm dying to fly a plane," she said. "I've had this dream in my heart for 20 years."

"Do it!"

"Go for it!"

"You can do it!"

Women called out their encouragement, and once again people clapped and shouted and laughed with joy.

After the break, the same woman approached me smiling. "I've just called a pilot-training school in my area," she said, clasping her hands together. "I'm so excited. I'm going to enroll in a program that begins next month. I'm shaking just thinking about it."

I was teary with happiness for her. She not only expressed her desire to all of us, but she also took action. I can imagine her now soaring across the sky, seated in front of the control panel of a small plane.

During the late-morning session, someone called out to me, "What's your next goal? What fun thing do you want to do that you've never done before?"

I didn't expect that. I had to think about it for a moment. I had hiked to the top of Mount Whitney. I had become a published writer. I had learned to ice-skate. I knew how to swim, row a boat, pedal a bike and speak in public without being scared. What was left?

I looked around for a moment while the women egged me on to share one thing I hadn't done before that I really wanted to do. And it had to be fun. I turned to the women's band behind me, and it suddenly hit me.

"I'd love to play the drums."

I had so enjoyed watching the female drummer during worship time. She put her heart and soul into her art. It looked like fun to me.

Everyone cheered me on. Later we broke for lunch. I stayed behind to speak with the drummer. "I'd like to surprise the ladies when we return from lunch by playing the drums during one song. Would you be okay with that? Would you teach me what to do?" My heart pounded so loud that I thought the sound would overwhelm even the drums.

"Absolutely," she said, smiling broadly. "Meet me back here 20 minutes before the afternoon session begins."

And so I did. I took my very first drum lesson that afternoon. Then we opened with worship, and I stepped up to the drums. The band played, "Jesus Loves Me, This I Know," to a beat I could keep up with. At first, I was a jumble of hands and feet, sticks and pedals, but soon I got the hang of it. I made it all the way through to the last beat. I breathed a sigh of relief, and the women stood up and cheered.

I had declared my desire. I took a risk. I followed it through. And I had *fun!* I wouldn't trade that experience for anything.

If I can live a new dream, so can you. You can do that thing you've always wanted to do—and have fun doing it. Decide what it is, and then get going!

GRACE
Well done, good and faithful servant! You have
been faithful with a few things; I will put you
in charge of many things.
(Matthew 25:23)

GRATITUDE
*Lord, I am grateful for the opportunity to keep dreaming
and desiring and doing—regardless of my age.*

GRIT
Today, I will come up with one thing
I haven't done that I've always wanted to
do and then take action.

Laughing Matters

My husband looked at an album of photos from my childhood. "You were so serious," he said. "Where were your dimples?"

I laughed as he pinched my cheek. Out they popped. Then I browsed the collection of pictures and noticed how somber I was in most of them—even at a birthday party or on vacation at Lake Wauconda. It seemed I was shy about laughing, even smiling, or maybe I didn't think I had anything to laugh about. I didn't know then what I know now: Laughing matters.

Dr. Tracy Gaudet, one of the premier women's physicians in the country, reports that researchers have found that laughter actually aids our immune systems to fight viruses and cancers, and it can help lower high blood pressure and decrease heart strain.

A friend of mine began doing stand-up comedy in order to add levity to his stressful life. He's now visiting comedy clubs a few nights a week to enjoy other comedians and to polish his own routine. He claims to feel better physically and emotionally by simply telling jokes and seeing people laugh.

My daughters tell me that they've never heard me laugh more than when I'm with my quick-witted son, Jim, who is a great comedian, mimic and jokester. Maybe in TV land everybody loves Raymond, but in real life, everybody loves Jim—because he knows how to make people laugh.

I also laugh a lot when I'm with my grandchildren. They bring out the kid in me, and together we're a bunch of sillies, dancing to loud music, playing tag, chasing each other down the street (they win as I stop to pant for breath) and reading funny stories.

"They give me life," says my husband, Charles. "I feel like a youngster again when I'm around them."

I remember my grandfather chuckling over my antics when I was a child, after a good story or during a funny film. He always seemed to wear a smile. When my mother (his daughter) got too serious or worried or upset about something in the family, he'd stop her, put a hand on her shoulder and remind her, "Eva, relax. You're taking life too seriously. Smile." And she would.

The great British evangelist and preacher C. H. Spurgeon, known for his serious pursuit of holy living, was also quite a cutup. He had a great sense of humor and did nothing to hide it.

Spurgeon laughed at comical incidents in life, at amusing elements of nature, even at his critics. He loved to share a wholesome joke with friends and colleagues and to include humorous stories in his sermons. William Williams, a fellow pastor and friend to Spurgeon, especially during the late years of Spurgeon's life, wrote of his friend's great mirth:

> What a bubbling fountain of humour Mr. Spurgeon had! I laughed more, I verily believe, when in his company than during all the rest of my life besides. He had the most fascinating gift of laughter . . . and he had also the greatest ability for making all who heard him laugh with him. When someone blamed him for saying humourous things in his ser-

mons, he said, "He would not blame me if he only knew how many of them I keep back."[1]

Imagine how your life would improve if you didn't take yourself or others so seriously but instead, like my grandfather and C. H. Spurgeon, discovered for yourself that laughing matters and can sometimes make the difference between life and death.

GRACE

A cheerful heart is good medicine, but a crushed spirit dries up the bones. (Proverbs 17: 22)

GRATITUDE

Lord, I thank You for the gift of laughter and the benefit it is to my health and to my perspective on life.

GRIT

Today, I will smile more, laugh more, and share more of who I really am.

Note

1. William Williams, "Personal Remembrances of Charles Haddon Spurgeon" (London: Passmore and Alabaster, 1895), p. 24, quoted in Larry J. Michael, "The Medicine of Laughter: Spurgeon's Humor," The Prayer Foundation. http://prayerfoundation.org/spurgeons_humor_larry_michael.htm (accessed March 18, 2006).

Daffodilly

For me, springtime means daffodils. I pick up a small bunch each week at the grocery store for 99 cents.

Of course, they're not much to look at sitting in a plain bucket without water at the end of the checkout counter. One could easily mistake the five or six flowers with their long green stalks and white heads hidden in a pale sheath for a bunch of green onions bound together with a plain rubber band. But once I take them away from the noise and glare of the market, bring them home to my sunny kitchen and plunge them into a vase of water, they open up into a golden bouquet that lasts an entire week.

I can't be sad or mad around a daffodil. I can only be glad. It reminds me of the true joy and pleasure one can have by simply *being*. There is nothing for a daffy to do except *be*. Yet this quiet beauty speaks to me every morning and spills sunshine across my day, reminding me to bloom where I am planted, to be expectant and thankful for the gift of life—however many days I have—and to express my true self regardless of my surroundings.

Like the lilies of the field, daffodils "do not labor or spin" (Matt. 6:28). They simply *are*, and yet their heavenly Father cares for them. How much more must He care for me, for you—for all His creatures, great and small?

This week when I pick up a box of tea bags, a bag of almonds, a sack of potatoes and a bottle of Essential Greens, I'll grab three bouquets of daffodils—one for the kitchen counter, one for my desk, and one for my bedside table. I'm already smiling as I think of the light and love they'll bring to each room.

I guess I could say I'm daffy over daffodils. They make a dilly of a bouquet, bringing fun and pleasure to my days and joy and humility to my spirit.

GRACE

Yet I tell you that not even Solomon in all his splendor was dressed like one of these.
(Matthew 6:29)

GRATITUDE

Lord, thank You for the gift of flowers and the pleasure and beauty they bring.

GRIT

Today, I will purchase a bouquet of flowers and place it in a lovely vase in a prominent place in my home where I can enjoy it each day.

The Good *New* Days

People love their stories, especially older people, and especially stories about "the good old days." There's even a magazine called *Good Old Days*. Nothing wrong with bygones, nostalgia, or looking back—unless you get stuck there. Many do. They start living in the past and neglect the good *new* days that are here to enjoy.

If you look back more often than you look forward, it might be time to consider what you're missing. Leslie Alderman, in her article "Get Happy" in *Real Simple* magazine, reminds readers that happiness (including having fun) brings its own reward. "It feels good—but it has another benefit: it's great for your health."[1]

Researchers who study the science of happiness, according to Alderman's report, have found that "happier people live longer, have stronger immune systems, and are more resilient to stress than their less sanguine counterparts."[2]

What are some of the simple things you can do to make the most of the good new days, to have more fun, more pleasure, more relaxation? Start by making subtle changes in your daily life. Keep your to-do list under control. You don't need to vacuum every day. You could change your linens twice a month instead of once a week. Cut down your volunteer activities. Which one do you really enjoy? Focus on that and let the others go.

Make sure you have plenty of "funshine" in your life each day. Do at least one thing that makes you happy. Don't let other people manipulate you into doing what is fun for them—at your expense. Treat yourself as a loving friend.

If you want to take a nap, go for it. If you love to walk your dog and chat with people you meet along the way, do that. If your pleasure comes from sewing, turn on your machine at least a few hours a week and pull out the fabric. If that means letting the dishes slide or letting your bed go unmade for a few hours, so be it. Fun is as important as a tidy kitchen or beautiful bedroom.

If you relax with classical music or a good book or find pleasure in pruning your roses and arranging a bouquet, choose that, and make it an essential part of your routine. Spending time with people you love, laughing, walking and keeping up with a hobby are just a few simple ways to help you remain interested in the good new days and to remain interesting to others.

As one woman said to her husband, who focuses on watching movies and reading books about World War II, "The war is over and we won! Now let's go dancing." I'm with her. We can learn from the past. We can be grateful for it. But we're here now, and it's time to step into the present and be part of it.

Right now, jot down 10 things you can do to add more fun to your life. Here are some ideas to consider:

1. Enroll in an art or writing class, even if you're unsure of your talent. You might be surprised.
2. Prepare a picnic with a friend, spouse or grandchild. Bring a ball and a Frisbee.
3. Join the YMCA or a local gym. Choose an exercise class that sounds like fun.
4. Take out four books from the local library and read one each week this month.

5. Climb into bed earlier than usual. Listen to some music and just breathe.
6. Make a pot of tea or a pitcher of lemonade. Sit in the yard, sip and relax.
7. Invite a friend to join you for a concert, lecture or tour of a museum.
8. Join a hiking, bird-watching or flower club and get close to nature.
9. Plan a trip to a place you've always wanted to see.
10. Buy yourself a single rose every Friday.

Raise your happiness quotient by including fun in your life—regardless of how you were raised, the messages you received about work when you were young, your current age, or what others think or say. It's your life—God's gift to you—to respect, cherish and live in the moment. These are the good new days. They are yours to enjoy.

GRACE
May the righteous be glad and rejoice before God;
may they be happy and joyful.
(Psalm 68:3)

GRATITUDE
I thank You, dear Lord, for the gift of play and for the opportunities to indulge in it, regardless of my age.

GRIT
Today, I will spend at least 30 minutes doing something playful, fun and refreshing.

Notes
1. Leslie Alderman, "Get Happy," *Real Simple* (September 2005), n.p.
2. Ibid.

Other Books by
Karen O'Connor

Squeeze the Moment
Making the Most of Life's Gifts and Challenges

Help, Lord! I'm Having a Senior Moment
Notes to God on Growing Older

Help, Lord! I'm Having a Senior Moment—*Again!*
Laughing Through the Realities of Growing Older

For more information, please write to
karen@karenoconnor.com

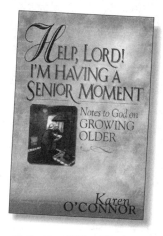

Make the Most of Every Moment

Squeeze the Moment
Making the Most of Life's Gifts and Challenges
Karen O'Connor
ISBN 08307.38363

Some women seem to be born with a joyful outlook. Others have to work at it. But joy can be a part of any woman's life, regardless of the circumstances. What does it take to live a life of joy? It starts with "doing good" toward one's self as well as others, taking care of physical and mental needs in a way that sparks well-being and happiness, tending to those areas of life that challenge us—even when we don't feel like it— without complaining, and ending each day with thanksgiving. *Squeeze the Moment* shows you how to look at your life in a fresh way and to squeeze your moments—the happy ones, the tragic ones, the predictable and unexpected ones—for all they're worth. Those who do are sure to find the treasure that each moment contains

Regal
God's Word for Your World™